A Prescription for a
Deeper Experience with God

THE HEART OF THE PROBLEM

Henry Brandt & Kerry L. Skinner

Foreword by Henry Blackaby

BROADMAN
& HOLMAN
PUBLISHERS

Nashville, Tennessee

© 1995
by Henry Brandt and Kerry L. Skinner
All rights reserved
Printed in the United States of America

4261-85
0-8054-6185-X

Dewey Decimal Classification: 153.4
Subject Heading: Problem Solving—Religious Life \ Christian Life

Library of Congress Cataloging-in-Publication Data
Brandt, Henry and Skinner, Kerry L.
    The heart of the problem / by Henry Brandt and Kerry L. Skinner.
        p.   cm.
    ISBN 0-8054-6185-X
                                                                    CIP

Contents

UNIT 8

UNIT 9

UNIT 10

UNIT 11

UNIT 12

Foreword

There comes to every child of God, and to every person, a wonderful word from God. It touches the deepest needs in the human experience—peace in the heart and in the entire life. "May the God of peace . . . equip you with everything good for doing his will, and may he work in us what is pleasing to him, through Jesus Christ, to whom be glory for ever and ever" (Heb. 13:20–21, NIV).

Henry Brandt has done a great service to the earnest, seeking heart by doing two things:

1. Confronting us with ourselves, and often at our most difficult and bewildering moments.
2. Confronting us with God's clear provision for our every condition.

He deals with tenderness, yet transparent truthfulness in some of the most significant factors in our lives: peace, joy, anger, bitterness, facing crises, forgiveness, sin, honesty, and interpersonal relationships.

In doing so, Brandt returns us again and again to the only place we can turn to—God, His Word (the Bible), the Holy Spirit, prayer and faith.

The world, and even well-meaning Christians, will share counsel that is not from God. What kind of response should there be? There should be a clear and resounding turning to God through the Scriptures and a confident trust in Him.

There is no doubt that Brandt has tested and proved God's ways and faithful provision in his own life! Sharing out of the depths of his own crises, his time with missionaries and the tender moments with those who have sought his counsel, he brings light and affirmation from real life to the counsels of God. He shares the Scriptures and shows from real life experiences how faithful God is to those whose hearts are right with Him.

We have too much of the "world's counsel and reasoning" as a substitute for God's counsel and truth. Brandt presents a refreshing and much-needed "return to God!"

Much practical help is gained from the format and the thought-provoking questions provided by Kerry L. Skinner. His years as associate pastor and minister of education, guiding God's people into a daily relationship with Jesus Christ, add much to the personalizing and putting into life the truth given by Brandt.

This material can be missed if read without thinking. Great truths, presented in clear, simple language and illustrations, can be overlooked. Read it slowly and thoughtfully! Pause, reflect, and meditate on each day's thoughts. Then, faithfully seek the enabling of God's Spirit to bring you to God's fullness in Jesus Christ. Live life as Jesus promised, in His peace and His joy!

"As the Father has loved me, so have I loved you. Now remain in my love. If you obey my commands, you will remain in my love, just as I have obeyed my Father's commands and remain in his love. I have told you this so that my joy may be in you and that your joy may be complete" (John 15:9–11, NIV).

This study guide, whether studied personally or in small groups, is most timely for our day! God will use Brandt's faithful witness and earnest pleas to return to God on His revealed terms as an instrument for revival among His people and spiritual awakening in our land.

Henry T. Blackaby

How Do I Use This Book?

This workbook is based on the book with the same title . . . *The Heart of the Problem,* formerly *When You're Tired of Treating the Symptoms and You're Ready for a Cure, Give Me a Call.*

Henry Brandt and Kerry L. Skinner have worked closely together for two years on how to apply this material to our lives and teach it to others. One result is this workbook. It is entirely the work of Kerry L. Skinner.

Reading the book is like driving a car. You can vary the speed as one scene after another passes by.

Using the workbook is like walking along a path. The scene passes by slowly. You can stop and rest or look closely at something that catches your eye.

Just as the freeway and the path have their places, so the book and the workbook have their places. The book gives you an uninterrupted view. The workbook allows you to leisurely absorb and drink deeply of many biblical principles.

For example, chapter one of the book is twenty-two pages. You can read it easily in one setting. It takes five days, except for unit one, to go through a unit in the workbook.

Would you like to make "lasting changes" in your life? Changes that give you victory over continuous difficulties in your life? This book is designed to help you work through your difficulties, make "lasting changes," and share with others how to practice these principles.

So how do you use this book? As you read, follow the guideline of reading one day of material at a time. Each day is marked with and followed by the subject for the day. Five days of material are included in each week or unit. Read each day's material during your quiet time of the day. As you are reading, follow these guidelines:

1. Complete the questions and learning activities.
2. Reflect on your answers and thoughts each day. Be honest with God about your heart.
3. Pray every day that God will give you new insights into making "lasting changes."
4. After you complete the five days of material, use the other two days of the week to reflect on other Bible passages that relate to that particular week's

study. A Bible concordance or topical Bible would be of great help in finding other passages.

5. Share what you are learning with a friend. Pray with them, asking God to help you discover "The heart of the problem."

You may also be asking, Do I use this as a self-study, small group study, or large group learning experience?

The answer is yes to all. You can use this book for a self-study.

However, small groups of twelve or less are great settings for using this material. Simply ask each person to do one week of assignments and then get together for a time of discussion and testimony about what God is doing in your life.

Large groups also work well. In this setting a competent large group speaker is needed to digest the material and teach the group once a week. Each participant should have a copy of the material. Participants do their work through the week and then attend the session where further study is shared by the large group leader.

I pray God will teach you great and marvelous truths that will help you make "lasting changes" as you discover the heart of the problem.

Kerry L. Skinner

Introduction

I have observed that individuals who move effectively through the ups and downs of life are regular church-goers. The weekly sermon, the Sunday School program, the musical program, the educational program, and Christian fellowship all help. Consistent partaking of such helps and practicing the teaching will provide strength for each day.

One of the most productive activities I have observed is group study. It works best at a retreat but is most worthwhile in a series like this study. I am convinced that an unseen hand guides the makeup of the group. There is a beginning and an end to the study. The teaching of the lesson, questions directed to the teacher, small-group discussions, conversations with individuals in the group, Bible memorization, and personal think time all help to fix the message in your mind.

The people who get the most out of this study tend to follow a pattern.

1. They want help. This illustrates a biblical condition: "Blessed are those who hunger and thirst for righteousness, for they shall be filled" (Matt. 5:6, NKJV).

2. The teaching stimulates discussion of biblical principles. This illustrates another biblical truth: "For the word of God is living and active. Sharper than any double-edged sword, it penetrates even to dividing soul and spirit, joints and morrow; it judges the thoughts and attitudes of the heart" (Heb. 4:12, NIV).

3. Acting on biblical principles result in lasting change and deepening fellowship. This illustrates another principle: "But if we walk in the light, as He is in the light, we have fellowship with one another, and the blood of Jesus Christ His Son cleanses us from all sin" (1 John 1:7, NKJV).

4. Continuous exposure to biblical principles illustrates your allegiance: "Then you will know the truth, and the truth will set you free" (John 8:32, NIV).

Jesus had a fascinating understanding and approach to people:

He knew their thoughts (Luke 11:17, KJV)
He knew their hypocrisy (Mark 12:15, KJV)

God knew their hearts (Acts 15:8, KJV)
He didn't need a case history.

Jesus knew that *the heart of the problem was the problem of the heart.*

Henry Brandt

UNIT ONE

The Myth of Complexity

Thought Starter:

What do you say? God is, or God isn't?

◆

Memory Verse for the Week:

But I fear, lest somehow, as the serpent deceived Eve by his craftiness, so your minds may be corrupted from the simplicity that is in Christ.
2 Corinthians 11:3, NKJV

DAY ONE

The Word that God speaks is alive and active: it cuts more keenly than any two-edged sword: it strikes through to the places where soul and spirit meet, to the innermost intimacies of a man's being: it exposes the very thoughts and motive's of a man's heart.

HEBREWS 4:12, PHILLIPS

Why Are So Many Christians Unhappy?

What I teach across the world is based on forty years of Bible memorization and reflection. Acting on these insights has been life-changing for me and my clients. My counseling career began in 1942 when, as a twenty-six-year-old engineer, the Holy Spirit tamed my vicious temper. People who knew me marveled at the change. Some of them asked if I could help them. With zero knowledge of the Bible, my wife and I gathered Bible verses useful for my friends and me. Two in particular caught my attention:

Blessed is the man . . . [whose] delight is in the law of the Lord; and in his law doth he meditate day and night. (Ps. 1:1–2, KJV)

Those who love Thy law have great peace, And nothing causes them to stumble. (Ps. 119:165, NASB)

To obey biblical guidelines as I lived out my life, I needed these guidelines in my head. For me, this clearly meant Bible memorization. Even now, forty years later, I still consider Bible memorization the single most important aid in my Christian life and in my counseling.

During the challenging years of obtaining a doctorate in this field, I listened to hundreds of stories from all levels of life and economic backgrounds. During those years, I studied with a secular textbook in one hand and a Bible in the other. I saw a wide gulf between the two approaches.

◆

Pause here and review the three preceding Bible verses. What are the benefits of Bible study? (Fill in the blanks)

- ◆ The Bible . . . exposes the very _____ and _____ of a man's heart. (Heb. 4:12)
- ◆ _____ is the man whose delight is in the law of the Lord. (Ps.1:1)
- ◆ _____ _____ have they who love your law and _____ can make them stumble. (Ps. 119:165)

Look up Matthew 24:35 and 2 Timothy 3:16. Jesus is speaking:

- ◆ Heaven and earth will pass away but _____ _____ will never pass away. (Matt. 24:35)
- ◆ All scripture is God-breathed and is useful for _____, _____, _____ and _____ in righteousness. (2 Tim. 3:16)

God's healing love can transform the most miserable life into one of comfort, joy, and deep personal peace. In the following pages notice the relief available through people helping people, through human efforts apart from God. Then, explore the many dimensions of Christ, the Cure: God's healing love can transform the most miserable life into one of comfort, joy, and deep personal peace.

I recommend that you memorize the verse at the beginning of each chapter. Think about the verse for a week or two:

- ♦ Recall the verse as often as possible.
- ♦ Examine what the verse means to you.
- ♦ Discuss the verse with others.
- ♦ Observe yourself in relation to the verse.
- ♦ Compare the verse to what you hear on radio and TV, in conversations and sermons.
- ♦ Compare the verse with what you read in books, magazines, and newspapers.
- ♦ Find other Bible verses that are similar.

Ten verses in your head at the end of this book are much better than a hundred pages in your notebook. Don't rush.

Hopefully, as you read the following pages, these lessons that I have collected from forty-plus years of living will help you along your way. Remember, you have a choice: relief or cure.

—*Henry Brandt*

Examine the Scriptures and/or your answers in today's lesson. Determine the most meaningful thought for you today. (Below is an example. After today, you should write in your answers each day.) Write your thought for the day here:

I will have to learn to think Bible.

Applying what God is pointing out to you is essential. How will you apply this truth to your life today?

I will memorize Psalm 1:1-2 and pay attention to what occupies my mind.

Write a short prayer to God that summarizes your thoughts.

Show me how to keep your Word in the forefront of my thinking.

Did God bring to mind someone who needs to hear this truth? Who?

My wife.

Thought for the Day:
The Scriptures will guide you to a cure.

♦

DAY TWO

God Is Able

In late 1947 I enrolled in graduate school, and for the first time in my life I was taught by highly trained, thoughtful, dedicated professors who not only used textbooks that ruled out God, but who themselves sincerely believed there is no God. For them, God isn't.

In my studies in clinical psychology, we grappled with the challenge of helping disturbed people. We thoughtfully pondered how to help hostile, hateful, resentful, rebellious, frustrated, confused, angry, cruel, selfish, dishonest, destructive people.

We all agreed that these words accurately described the dark side of human behavior. We were taught that a person is a biological organism whose total personality is the product of functioning in a social and cultural context.

A disturbed person is one whose needs are not met when he or she comes into the world. It is a person who is neglected, a person who lives in an environment that is cold and indifferent. To understand what is behind this disturbed person's behavior is to seek complex origins in a murky past. The process can take months or years. Then the question becomes: What in the world can be changed or given to release this person from a prison of destructive emotions and behavior?

"No deity can save us. We must save ourselves."

This is the position taken in secular colleges, secular textbooks, in most graduate training, and in a formidable mass of "scientific research." This is the operating philosophy of government, heavily financed mental health agencies, professionally trained counselors, and the bulk of medically trained personnel.

Human problems are not ignored. In fact, we spend billions of dollars annually searching for solutions. Educators, politicians, psychiatrists, psychologists, sociologists, social workers, social agencies, and law enforcement agencies confront these problems every day.

A massive group of people—intelligent, educated, influential, politically powerful people—who have the best interests of humanity at heart, firmly and fiercely reject the concept of sin, a creator, and a God. You might compare that host of people to a huge giant called Goliath. They firmly believe: God isn't.

Then there is another tiny group standing up to Goliath. This group (and I am one of them) believes that God is. We agree with the Goliath crowd that these words accurately describe the dark side of human behavior (hostile, hateful, resentful, rebellious, frustrated, confused, angry, cruel, selfish, dishonest, destructive).

But at this point in the road we come to a fork. We disagree that these words describing human behavior are socially and culturally caused. Our guidebook is the Bible. This book puts all those descriptive words under one heading. The heading is Sin.

In the Bible, Jesus commented on the nature of people: "What comes out of a man is what makes him 'unclean.' For from within, out of men's hearts, come evil thoughts, sexual immorality, theft, murder, adultery, greed, malice, deceit, lewdness, envy, slander, arrogance and folly. All these evils come from inside and make a man 'unclean'" (Mark 7:20–23).

The apostle Paul gives us a description of our sinful nature. "Sexual immorality, impurity and debauchery; idolatry and witchcraft; hatred, discord, jealousy, fits of rage, selfish ambition, dissensions, factions and envy; drunkenness, orgies, and the like"(Eph. 5:19–21).

We are born with sinful hearts. Society only brings out of our hearts what is already there. When our leader announced to the Goliath crowd that He came to save them from their sins, they replied with one thunderous voice: Crucify Him. They did.

In standing up to Goliath our little group might be compared to a little boy called David. We dare to use the word sin and affirm there is no human remedy for sin. We believe a Savior is needed who will cleanse us from sin and empower us to walk in the Spirit (in love, joy, peace, long-suffering, kindness, goodness, faithfulness, gentleness, and self-control).

If it is sin, that's good news. Sin is the simplest thing in the world to deal with. Jesus died to cleanse us from sin.

"Too simple," says the Goliath crowd.

◆

Locate 1 John 3:4 in your Bible. How does this verse define sin?

_____

_____

Write your definition of sin:

_____

_____

It is recorded that the third day after Jesus was crucified, the disciples were assembled in a room with the doors shut for fear of the religious leaders. Jesus appeared in the room and said to them, "Peace be with you." Then He breathed on them and said, "Receive the Holy Spirit" (John 20:21–22, NASB).

Do you believe that Jesus can change a fearful person into a peaceful person as quickly as it takes to exhale a breath of air? Check your response.

- ◆ No, Jesus does not want to heal people that quickly.
- ◆ No, I don't believe Jesus would give people an escape that easily. He wants to work through all of their problems slowly.
- ◆ I believe Jesus can heal quickly, but most people will not allow Him to help.
- ◆ If I confess my sin and repent, Jesus will forgive and cleanse me immediately.

Make no mistake. The people who approach life from humanistic assumptions make up a huge majority of the people you deal with every day. How long has it been since you had a conversation about sin and its cure?

You need to expand your knowledge of sin so that you know how Jesus can help you. This workbook will instruct you how to live free from the bondage of sin and empower you to enjoy the fruit of the Spirit.

Look up each of these references and read the complete verse:

- ◆ [Jesus] knowing their thoughts (Luke 11:17, KJV)

◆ Jesus knowing their hypocrisy (Mark 12:15, NASB)
◆ God knows your hearts (Acts 15:8, NASB)

Jesus didn't need a case history. He knows our hearts.

Write your response to this statement: "Jesus knows far better than anyone else what is going on in my life. Therefore, through the Word, Jesus is the best one to turn to for real healing."

_____

_____

_____

God does not bring Scripture to mind that has never been studied or memorized. Make sure you spend time hiding God's Word in your mind.

There are six things the Lord hates, seven that are detestable to him: haughty eyes, a lying tongue, hands that shed innocent blood, a heart that devises wicked schemes, feet that are quick to rush into evil, a false witness who pours out lies and a man who stirs up dissension among brothers.
PROVERBS 6:16–19, NIV

Examine the Scriptures and/or your answers in today's lesson. Determine the most meaningful thought for you today. Write that thought for the day here:

_____

_____

_____

Applying what God is pointing out to you is essential. How will you apply this truth to your life today?

_____

_____

Write a short prayer to God that summarizes your thoughts.

_____

_____

_____

_____

Did God bring to mind someone who needs to hear this truth? Who?

_____

Thoughts for the Day:

There is no human remedy for sin.

————

If it is sin that is the problem, that's good news! It is the simplest thing in the world to deal with. Jesus died to cleanse us from sin.

————

God is able to cure you from your problem of sin.

◆

DAY THREE

The Spirit's Life Is the Best Life!

Once, when I came upon this hopeful statement: "For the Lord gives wisdom; from His mouth come knowledge and understanding" (Prov. 2:6, NASB), I began to pray for wisdom and understanding. Over a period of months I experienced some amazing encounters and results with people seeking help. I can't claim credit because my input was often very minor.

Examine some of these experiences of people who have come to me with their burdens. You be the judge if the stories over the next days are too simple.

————

He must have been in his early forties. She looked a bit younger. She held a little baby, perhaps two months old. They had anticipated this week-long family conference situated in a wooded area beside a clear, large lake.

Tragedy had marred the last year. Their four-year-old daughter died after a lingering illness. Soon after the next pregnancy, both his family and her family gathered at the hospital for the results of an ultrasound test to determine the sex of their unborn second child. Expecting an exciting announcement, the whole family was shocked when a somber doctor stated that the baby she was carrying was dead.

It was a heavy Christmas that year. Very few of their friends stood with them. They faced their sorrow alone. Even the progress of a third pregnancy and new son's birth had not eased their pain.

If you had been with this couple at that time, how would you have consoled them?

_____

_____

We were two days into the family conference. They were not enjoying themselves as they had hoped. The double deaths a year ago haunted them here with all the other families together in the dining room. He was also burdened with the recent failure of a business relationship which left him with a large financial obligation.

Could I help them? He sat there with clenched teeth behind tight lips. She held on to her little baby with a look of desperation.

How could anyone bear such trouble? No glib answer would magically remove their burdens.

I had to make a decision The answer seemed clear to me. However, my guess was that they weren't ready to talk about answers; they were too preoccupied with their problems. I encouraged and prayed with them for an open mind as they attended the meetings.

As one of the conference speakers, my emphasis was on forgiving others of their trespasses whether they asked for forgiveness or not, or even if you never saw them again. Nursing a grudge within your own mind hurts no one else but you. You are a slave to the person you hate. Jesus said, "If you forgive men their trespasses, your heavenly Father will also forgive you. But if you do not forgive men their trespasses, neither will your Father forgive your trespasses" (Matt. 6:14–15, NKJV).

The other speaker taught the Book of Galatians. The acts of the sinful nature block the fruit of the Spirit. The barrier is made out of sexual immorality, hatred, discord, fits of rage, jealousy, selfish ambition, dissensions, and envy.

Think about the acts of the sinful nature. Check the words below that you believe are the acts of the sinful nature.

- ◆ Love
- ◆ Jealousy
- ◆ Hatred
- ◆ Kindness
- ◆ Peace

- ◆ Selfish ambition
- ◆ Anger
- ◆ Hope
- ◆ Bitterness
- ◆ Joy

What does it mean to be filled by the Spirit? _____

_____

Look up Galatians 5:22–23. These verses say, "But the fruit of the Spirit is love, joy, peace, patience, kindness, goodness, faithfulness, gentleness and self-control."

Which would you rather have as a life-style, the fruit of the Spirit or the works of the flesh? _____

To be filled by the Spirit means to be controlled by the Spirit. It is necessary to be filled with the Spirit in order to live the Christian life. "Why would anyone turn their back on an inner life like that?" the speaker asked.

Two days later the couple visited me. Their clenched teeth and tight lips had been replaced with radiant smiles. They dropped in to tell me that they listened and got their answers. They had dealt with their own sins. They didn't need to talk to me anymore. Besides, they had to get to the lakeside to enjoy the afternoon.

What do you think the couple did to change from tight lips to a radiant smile?

_____

_____

Three months later, I received a phone call from them. All was well; he and his partner had resolved their differences.

It was a very complex problem, and I apparently had little to do with the solution. This was God's doing, not mine. Was this too simple? We must be careful not to underestimate the help available to hungry, open-minded Christians from a prayer-filled conference.

How do you think Matthew 6:14–15 applied to this couple? _____

_____

Watch for advertisements that offer a life-style with results similar to the fruit of the Spirit. List your findings here: _____

_____

_____

Examine the Scriptures and/or your answers in today's lesson. Determine the most meaningful thought for you today. Write your thought for the day here:

_____

_____

_____

_____

Applying what God is pointing out to you is essential. How will you apply this truth to your life today? _____

_____

_____

Write a short prayer to God that summarizes your thoughts._____

_____

_____

_____

Did God bring to mind someone who needs to hear this truth? Who?

_____

Thought for the Day:

Why would anyone turn his back on the great inner life developed by the fruit of the Spirit?

◆

DAY FOUR

If we confess our sins, he is faithful and just and will forgive us our sins and purify us from all unrighteousness.
1 JOHN 1:9, NIV

God's Cleansing Power

Joe and Martha enjoyed the growing-up years of their son, Mike. He had a fun personality and bright mind. However, in high school he began withdrawing from the family. They passed it off as a phase and figured it was due to peer pressure at school, but it only increased in his college years. At the age of twenty, while home for the summer, Mike's problem came to a head.

About 1:00 A.M. they received a phone call. Mike said, "You'd better come down here." He had been speeding while drunk with three buddies in the car. He missed a right turn, drove off the end of the street into a driveway, rear-ended a parked car, shoved it through the corner of the garage, and wrecked his own car beyond repair. Mike was arrested, charged with drunk driving, and was being held at the police station. They would not release him, so his father returned home about 2:30 A.M.

They could no longer ignore the fact that they had been putting 'Band-Aids' on the problem for a long time. Martha and Joe slept no more that night, facing the reality that their son had emotionally departed some time ago. Band-Aids would not work; major changes were needed now. They finally concluded that they loved Mike so much and were willing to do whatever was necessary to help, including fight for him.

Joe and Martha felt that Mike and his friends were not good for each other and the relationship should end. They feared that Mike might not accept this and he might leave home as a result.

They decided to stop him if he tried to leave; and if he did leave, to go after him. In order to lose their son, he would have to reject their love. It would not be because they didn't love him enough to fight for him.

His father had to face another tough truth. He knew what he should do, but he had no confidence; his track record was not good, and his judgment was too subjective.

Realizing how important it was for them to make the right decisions, they called me, an old friend who lived three thousand miles away in Florida.

We sat at the kitchen table while I asked questions and took notes. After about an hour and a half, I knew enough about their problem to be able to say what each one needed to hear. "Joe, you have been foolish and need to repent. You said you knew Mike was not going in the right direction, but compared to yourself at his age, he wasn't doing too bad. Since when were you, at that age, God's standard for anybody? You also said you didn't want to drive Mike away. Mike, did you know that your dad didn't want to drive you away?"

Mike nodded. "Martha, you have been foolish and need to repent. You have been trying to make your son happy. Stop playing God. Mike, did you know your mother wanted to make you happy?"

Mike nodded again.

◆

What can you think of that they did wrong? _____

_____

_____

Love requires a willingness to help. Can you think of a friend or family member who needs your help? Write their name(s) here: _____

_____

Would you be willing to speak the truth in love to them if God leads them to you?

_____

Look up these verses and decide how they apply to the rest of the story:

- The Lord _____ those he loves, as a father the son he delights in. (Prov. 3:12)

- _____ your son, and he will give you peace; he will bring delight to your soul. (Prov. 29:17)

- The rod of _____ imparts _____, but a child left to itself _____ his mother. (Prov. 29:15)

◆

Then I said, "Joe and Martha, you have a reasonably intelligent twenty-year-old son who has figured that his dad doesn't want to drive him away and that his mother wants to make him happy. He's been playing that for all it's worth.

"Your home has been a training center, but your son has been the trainer training his parents in the way he wants them to go. Allow what he wants, and he rewards you with a good attitude. Inhibit what he wants, and he penalizes you with a bad attitude. Your son has been controlling this home by his attitude."

I then turned to Mike. "Mike, you are an angry, deceitful young man. That's not my opinion but what you have revealed about yourself and I recorded it in my notes. I don't need to meet your friends to know what they're like. They're just like you—that's why they are your friends.

"Mike, if you don't repent, I predict that this is your future: You will find some attractive young woman who is just like you. You'll seem to have a lot in common, think you're in love, marry and then turn your anger and deceitfulness on each other and ruin each other's lives."

Looking at all three of them, I continued, "You each need to repent, but then you each need to change. You will each need help to change, and you will each resist the help you need. However, if you don't receive the help to change, you will revert into the habit patterns that made this mess in the first place."

After that I could only say, "Well, I can't repent for you, so you might as well take me to the airport."

Martha and Joe repented, but Mike seemed cold and unresponsive until a couple of days later. He seemed so matter-of-fact, saying that he had repented and never really meant to hurt his parents. Although they had difficulty believing him, they perceived the counsel they had received had the ring of truth.

They realized that in the fall Mike should enroll in a school that would provide the helpful environment he needed in order to change. Of course, Mike did not want that kind of school environment; he wanted to continue living off-campus, accountable to no one. Yet at the same time, Mike didn't want to continue as he had been.

He resisted; we persisted. Mike enrolled in a school with rules, living on campus in a dorm with "nosy dorm leaders."

Their family struggled through a number of tear-filled times, but they didn't give up.

◆

Are you facing a problem or need that requires a change in your life? Write your thoughts concerning the change you are desiring:_____

_____

_____

What kind of energies are you using to solve your problem?_____

_____

_____

Are you willing to change?   Yes, ❑   No ❑

Search out some Bible verses to support your decisions.

◆

Imagine their surprise when, after getting his bachelor's in English, Mike decided to stay in the same school (with rules) and to pursue another degree in counseling. He chose another school (with rules) for his master's in counseling and then gained his doctorate at one of the leading universities in the nation. He is now married to a lovely Christian, and they are about to have their first child.

The core problem was even more with the parents than with their son. He was more willing to receive correction and direction than they had been able or willing to provide it.

Does such a brief encounter as I had with this family have lasting results? Well, this occurred ten years ago, and to date, all is well with Mike.

Do not underestimate the cleansing power available when anyone approaches God as a repentant sinner who has seen the sin and wants to be restored and renewed. It doesn't take God long to transform a humble person.

◆

Are you aware of a problem that you are trying to solve without God's help?

_____

Examine the Scriptures and/or your answers in today's lesson. Determine the most meaningful thought for you today. Write your thought for the day here:

_____

_____

_____

_____

Applying what God is pointing out to you is essential. How will you apply this truth to your life today? _____

_____

Write a short prayer to God that summarizes your thoughts._____

_____

_____

_____

Did God bring to mind someone who needs to hear this truth? Who?

_____

Thoughts for the Day:

Do not put "Band-Aids" on long-time problems.

———

Do not underestimate the cleansing power available when anyone approaches God as a repentant sinner who has seen the sin and wants to be restored and renewed.

———

It doesn't take God long to transform a humble person.

♦

DAY FIVE

Part One:
A Listener with an Open Heart

Duke is the pastor of a church today. It was not always so. He was a very strong-willed child from the day he was born. At age seventeen he was in complete rebellion. He used drugs, stole, was rude and obnoxious. His parents sought help from counselors, doctors, and the police, but none could help. He ran away from home for eleven weeks. Then he returned on his own. He continued his uncooperative, obnoxious ways. His father's job required travel, so his mother attempted to deal with her son. They restricted him to the house but he refused to comply, threatening to leave again.

I was speaking on family relations when an elegantly dressed lady approached me after one session and asked if I could help her. She told me this story. She had run out of ideas, not knowing what else to do.

Knowing how to respond to such a problem with so little information is very difficult. At a time like this I need to turn God-ward, admit my helplessness, and appeal to Him for wisdom. Theoretically, I need information; what is she like, what is her husband like, some history about Duke. Without proper information, how could I help?

My heart was filled with sympathy and compassion for this obviously desperate, anxious lady. It seemed logical to comfort her by reassuring her that it was quite normal to be anxious. However, that's not what I heard myself say. Instead, I told her that she had at least two problems, perhaps three.

First, she needed to relax.

♦

How do you see her problem? _____

_____

How would you help her calm down?_____

_____

_____

♦

Two Bible verses came to mind:

Trust in the Lord with all your heart,
and lean not on your own understanding;
In all your ways acknowledge Him,
and He shall direct your paths.
PROVERBS 3:5–6, NKJV

Let the peace of God rule in your hearts . . . and be thankful.
COLOSSIANS 3:15, NKJV

How can you tell if you are trusting in the Lord? Look up Philippians 4:6–7.
  ♦ Do not be anxious about anything, but in everything, by prayer and petition,
  with _____, present your _____ to God. And the
  _____ _____ _____, which transcends all _____, will
  guard your _____ and your_____ in Christ Jesus.

How do these verses speak to the changes needed in your life? _____

_____

_____

Are you trusting in the Lord with all your heart concerning this problem?
Yes, ❑   No ❑   Are you thankful for this situation?   Yes, ❑   No ❑

♦

Her response was total unbelief. How is it possible to calm down under these conditions and be thankful? I reminded her that to say the least, she could be thankful that she got a chance to be reminded that God would direct her path. She seemed more disturbed than ever.

Second, whatever she did about her son, she needed to be sure that she and her husband were like-minded about any action.

Third, I could not advise her specifically on what to do, but something, probably quite drastic, should be done quickly. I reminded her that she and her husband needed to trust the Lord and not be afraid of losing their son. They probably already had; this was the opportunity to win him back.

Do you agree with this advice?_____

What else might you suggest?_____

_____

_____

She left, looking more despondent than ever. A short conversation immediately after a meeting is hard to handle. This one surely looked like a dud. My intentions were good, but it seemed that the more I tried to help, the more agitated she became. One thing, however, I have learned is to depend upon a person's second reaction to a conversation rather than the first.

Several years later, a clean-cut young man came to the platform after a meeting and introduced himself. "

My name is Duke," he said. "I'm in college preparing for the ministry. I came to thank you for encouraging my parents not to give up on me."

Twenty years later, at another meeting, this same lady named Catherine and her husband Bob came up to me; although at first, I didn't recognize her. She gave me a report on Duke. He finished college and then seminary, where he married a fellow student. Today, the couple is pioneering in the opening of a new church.

Catherine told me what happened after she left the meeting twenty years ago. She did have a second reaction. She had to admit that she had not considered it even remotely possible to relax. She was at her wits end over what to do; professionals were no help. But she had not thought of turning the problem over to God and to consciously team up with her husband.

◆

Remember the problem you wrote on page 14? Locate two or three Scriptures that speak to the problem. Write the references and key ideas here:_____

_____

_____

_____

Have you seen the need to turn the problem over to God? Have you done that?

_____

◆

She and her husband renewed their commitment to do anything to save their son from sure destruction and to depend on God to direct their paths. Now Duke was up against two people renewed in their dedication to seek God's best for their son. They agreed to expect Duke to do what was right and to do whatever was necessary to enforce righteousness, whatever that means.

◆

Look up 1 Corinthians 1:10 and Proverbs 13:24.

◆ I appeal to you, brothers, in the name of our Lord Jesus Christ, that all of you _____ with _____ _____ so that there be no _____ among you and that you may be _____ united in mind and thought. (1 Cor. 1:10)

◆ He who spares the rod hates his son, but he who _____ him is careful to discipline him. (Prov. 13:24)

◆

A few days later, Duke and his father were in the kitchen, just the two of them. On the counter was a bottle of vitamins that his mother used. Duke wanted some of the vitamins. Bob was not sure if these were prescription drugs, so he told Duke to ask his mother for permission. Duke cursed his mother, and Bob rebuked his son sharply. Duke swung at his dad; Bob knocked him to the floor. A vigorous fight followed. Duke managed to get away and took off on his bicycle. Bob took after him in his car, but couldn't find him.

Bob returned home and went to Duke's room where he found a sizable quantity of marijuana. He went to the police station and swore out a warrant for his son's arrest.

Wow! Does this sound like the Lord directing Bob's path? This all took place on Mother's Day.

They accepted this crisis as God's leading. They were doing the best they knew how on behalf of their beloved son.

When Duke came home to pack up and leave, Catherine called the police. They arrived quickly, with not one but three cars with lights flashing, attracting the attention of the whole neighborhood. Two policemen arrested Duke on assault and battery, handcuffed him, and led him to a police car. Duke's sister and the neighbors were appalled.

The hearing was scheduled; bail was set high enough so that Duke's friends could not get him out for two weeks. Duke had bragged that the police would never catch him, but now he was in jail on a warrant sworn out by his own parents.

At the hearing Duke was sentenced to ten days in jail and one year of probation. While he was in jail, Duke refused to talk to his father. He would talk to his mother. She visited him and brought him reading material. While he served the ten days, a doctor discovered that Duke had a serious case of hypoglycemia.

When Duke began his probation, a police sergeant instructed him to fill out a daily report of his activities, accounting for each hour, and submit it weekly. He warned Duke that if he failed to submit the report, he would personally see to it that Duke would get a five-year sentence. He showed Duke the pictures of several young men who called his bluff and who were all in prison. Duke was paroled in the custody of his parents.

Catherine nursed Duke back to health. He continued to ignore his father, but complied with the terms of his probation.

When Duke regained his health he got a job with a contractor. It was a pick-and-shovel job, mostly with a partner. This fellow was annoyingly cheerful and considerate toward Duke. Day in and day out, week in and week out, this fellow lived a consistent, cheerful life. Every chance he got he tried to tell Duke about Jesus, who saved him from a life of anger and misery.

One day Duke said, "Mom, guess what happened to me." Her heart sank. What trouble is he in now? she thought.

"I gave my heart to Jesus," he said. "From now on I'm living for God."

Duke then made a dramatic U-turn. He went to places where he had stolen things and made restitution. He changed his friends and graduated from college and seminary.

Today he is pastor of a church and I had the pleasant surprise of having lunch with Duke recently. I asked him to tell me his memories of that period. Here are a few of his reflections:

> One day two giant policemen walked into my room at home and arrested me. Man, they were prepared. They surrounded the house. They had a dog in case I tried to run away. Guns and everything. I sat in jail for two weeks before getting out. But I didn't stop drugs, I just got smarter and more careful.
>
> I had a job working for a construction company with a pick and shovel with this long-haired hippie that kept talking about Jesus. One day we were in the bottom of an empty swimming pool shoveling out slimy scum. Man, it was the worst job I have ever had. Smelly, got all over you, yuck!
>
> We took a short rest break, and the fellow with whom I was working told me about Jesus. Now, a lot of things from that part of my life are a little confusing, having taken everything from LSD to you-name-it, but something clicked inside of me. What he said seemed to make sense. I went inside to wash my hands and face at lunch time. When I looked up at the mirror to dry my face, I felt clean. I knew something had happened. I went out and told my working buddy that I had become a Christian.
>
> Later, I told my drug friends about Jesus. They said, "Ahhh, you'll get over it. You're just going through a phase." Well, they may be right, but it's been over twenty years and I haven't gotten over it yet. You know, Dr. Brandt, there's another thing. I never quit doing drugs; I just didn't want them anymore.

Don't take too lightly the help that is available to a listener with an open heart. God had prepared a solution for that mother. Our brief encounter after a meeting had to be just a tiny part. My little advice motivated her to bring God in on the solution. It didn't seem very hopeful as she walked away from our little chat, but God's ways are not our ways.

♦

Locate Jeremiah 33:3 in your Bible.

♦ Call to me and I will _____ you and tell you _____ and _____ things you do not know.

Ask God to give you a chance to listen to someone and depend on God to give a suggestion.

Examine the Scriptures and/or your answers in today's lesson. Determine the most meaningful thought for you today. Write that thought here: _____

_____

_____

_____

Applying what God is pointing out to you is essential. How will you apply this truth to your life today? _____

_____

Write a short prayer to God that summarizes your thoughts._____

_____

_____

_____

Did God bring to mind someone who needs to hear this truth? Who?_____

_____

Thoughts for the Day:

Depend on a person's second reaction to a conversation
rather than the first.

———

Don't take too lightly the help that is available when you turn to God and
ask Him to guide you to a solution.

♦

DAY FIVE

Part Two:
Give Simplicity a Chance

Tim Daley is a biblical counselor. We have compared notes for years. Four hundred men were at a retreat that he invited me to attend. I was to learn that thirty-five of them were there because his life had touched their lives.

Bert was one of the men at this conference. He had set up certain procedures for the insurance agents who worked for him to follow. One agent who refused to comply was Bert's older brother.

Over the next year they had many strained conversations about the issue, which became more and more heated. One day when they were angrily throwing verbal bricks at each other, his brother cleaned out his office and left. Bert called him a few days later. The verbal barrage continued until, finally, Bert hung up on his brother. He was livid with rage. There was no contact for a month.

Earlier, when his brother came to work for him, they had agreed that any problems would be worked out amiably and that work would not interfere with family ties. Yet here they were sharply divided and a major holiday coming up.

Finally Bert consulted with Tim Daley, who listened intently to the story. Tim leaned forward and said, "You are a bitter, angry man. The way you talked to your brother is unacceptable as a Christian example. You need to repent and then apologize to your brother for your bad attitude. You will not find peace until you do."

End of interview.

What do you think about Daley's approach? _____

_____

_____

Can you think of an example similar to this experience? _____

_____

♦

Bert wasn't prepared for Tim's response. He was expecting reassurance that he was justified in his attitude because of the problems his brother created.

He pondered Tim's advice. He was afraid to call his brother, but the idea plagued him. Bert was reluctant to admit that he was bitter, angry, and self-righteous. Finally he admitted this to God with a repentant heart and asked to be cleansed and empowered to love his brother. To his surprise, his resistance to calling his brother turned into an urge to see him.

His brother didn't want to see him, but Bert pleaded for a twenty-minute meeting. It was agreed to reluctantly, and they met at the appointed place. His brother said nothing, but Bert felt compassion toward him. He proceeded to apologize for the attitude he had toward his brother.Gone was the bitterness. He asked for forgiveness; his brother had tears in his eyes, as did Bert.

Bert said that at that moment it was as though a two-hundred-pound weight was lifted from his shoulders.

Years have passed. The problem is behind them. Allowing God to change his heart was the first step in changing a complex problem into a simple one. Bert was a repentant prayer away from a change of heart all the time.

There are many such stories happening every day. Jesus said: "Come to Me, all you who labor and are heavy laden, and I will give you rest." (Matt. 11:28, NKJV)

The psalmist said: "Cast your burden upon the Lord, and He will sustain you." (Ps. 55:22, NASB)

Is there something you know about that needs a change of heart? _____

_____

Think about these verses.

If your brother sins against you, go and show him his fault,just between the two of you.If he listens to you, you have won your brother over. But if he will not listen, take one or two others along, so that every matter may be established by the testimony of two or three witnesses. If he refuses to listen to them, tell it to the church; and if he refuses to listen even to the church, treat him as you would a pagan or a tax collector.

MATTHEW 18:15–17

Brothers, if someone is caught in a sin, you who are spiritual should restore him gently. But watch yourself, or you also may be tempted.
GALATIANS 6:1

Examine the Scriptures and/or your answers in today's lesson. Determine the most meaningful thought for you today. Write your thought for the day here:

_____

_____

_____

_____

Applying what God is pointing out to you is essential. How will you apply this truth to your life today? _____

_____

_____

Write a short prayer to God that summarizes your thoughts._____

_____

_____

_____

_____

Did God bring to mind someone who needs to hear this truth? Who?

_____

I often have people tell me, "Dr. Brandt, it's just not that simple!" My reply is, "Have you tried it?"

Long pause. End of discussion. Many argue with me on this point except my clients.

Thoughts for the Day:

Allowing God to change your heart is the first step in changing a complex problem into a simple one.

———

Many people are just a repentant prayer away from a change of heart.

◆

(Optional—But Recommended!)

Bring forward your thoughts from each day:

1. _____
2. _____
3. _____
4. _____
5. _____

Bring forward your application:

1. _____
2. _____
3. _____
4. _____
5. _____

Bring forward your prayers:

1. _____
2. _____
3. _____
4. _____
5. _____

Bring forward who you shared your thoughts with:

1. _____
2. _____
3. _____
4. _____
5. _____

Thought for the Week:

Give simplicity a chance!

♦

UNIT TWO

Peace and Satisfaction in This World?

Thought Starter:

Why are Christians not in the least embarrassed over
the absence of peace and rest in their lives?

◆

Memory Verse for the Week:

**These things I have spoken to you, that in Me you may have peace. In
the world you will have tribulation; but be of good cheer, I have
overcome the world.**

JOHN 16:33, NKJV

DAY ONE

Peace I leave with you, My peace I give to you; not as the world gives do I give to you. Let not your heart be troubled, neither let it be afraid.
JOHN 14:27, NKJV

Peace and Places

Jesus clearly tells us that it is His intention for us to move through this world peacefully and cheerfully, untroubled and unafraid as long as we look to Him to enable us. With such a resource readily available, I am overwhelmed by the absence of personal peace and by the level of misery under which Christians are willing to live. They don't seem the least bit embarrassed or hesitant to declare:

- ♦ "I'm under stress."
- ♦ "I'm pretty anxious."
- ♦ "I'm worried."
- ♦ "I'm angry!"

- ♦ "I'm so unhappy."
- ♦ "I can't get along with him (her)."
- ♦ "I'm afraid."

Christians often accept the word of secular mental health people who tell us that such conditions are socially and culturally caused and relief is to be found in the world. They are correct. Jesus Himself said you can find a kind of peace in the world. But He also said that we should look to Him, not to the world He created. I see many Christians adopt, without thinking, a So-what?-Never-mind-what-Jesus-said attitude and turn to the world in search of peace.

♦

Can you think of some places that have a calming influence over you? _____

_____

_____

Can you think of some places that should have been a calming influence but turned out to be disturbing? Why? _____

_____

_____

_____

Jesus tells us that He can cause us to move through this troubled world peacefully, cheerfully, untroubled, and unafraid:

> **These things I have spoken to you, that in Me you may have peace. In the world you will have tribulation; but be of good cheer, I have overcome the world.**
>
> JOHN 16:33, NKJV

Examine this verse. Do you believe you can experience real peace?_____

_____

Did Jesus say you could?_____

What will it require for you to experience this verse?_____

_____

_____

What will you do with Jesus and His words in this verse? He says you can have peace in this world by turning either to Him or to the world (your environment) that He created. Let's take a look at what the world offers first:

- ♦ Places
- ♦ Activities and events
- ♦ Things
- ♦ People

Wow! What a Beautiful Place!

I stepped out of the car at the Horn Creek Conference Center in the mountains near Colorado Springs and took a big breath of clean mountain air. The spectacular Rocky Mountains rimmed the valley where I stood.

We all know that feeling of traveling a long way and experiencing the anticipation and then the excitement of arrival; that's what I felt. Hiking in the mountains, walking beautiful trails, fishing in a stream, or just standing by a gorgeous waterfall are all a source of anticipated relaxation.

Recently I visited my son-in-law in Idaho. I sat in the living room and looked out over a golden grain field that extended out from the backyard. In the distance I could see the foothills rising to meet the clear Idaho sky. From the front porch you could see a pasture with sheep grazing. What a peaceful place this is!

Interacting alone with this magnificent creation can quiet one's heart. Unfortunately, conflict with one another, even in the most scenic places, will steal away that peace.

A couple experiencing serious marital problems was to go on a vacation somewhere. So the husband surprised his wife with a first-class deluxe Caribbean cruise. The drive to the boat dock was pleasant as they anticipated all the fun they would have on the ship for a week in the sun.

When they entered their small, narrow stateroom, the husband quickly changed into his loudest multi-colored shirt (which his wife intensely disliked), threw the first shirt on the floor in the corner (she liked to keep a neat house), and pressured his wife with, "Honey, will you please hustle it up!" (He liked to be on time and she was always late.) On the deck, he, being an extrovert, began to loudly introduce himself to people. She, being an introvert, was embarrassed by his loudness and his awful shirt. They both wanted to accomplish something in their relationship that they couldn't do at home. Needless to say, the Caribbean cruise was a disaster because they brought themselves along.

Sadly, we all know that peace inside an individual is not determined by being in a place.

♦

Can you identify a time when something outside of you disturbed you?

_____

_____

Examine the Scriptures and/or your answers in today's lesson. Determine the most meaningful thought for you today. Write that thought here: _____

_____

_____

Applying what God is pointing out to you is essential. How will you apply this truth to your life today? _____

_____

Write a short prayer to God that summarizes your thoughts._____

_____

_____

_____

Did God bring to mind someone who needs to hear this truth? Who?

_____

◆

Thoughts for the Day:

Sadly, we all know that peace inside an individual is not determined by being in a place.

———————

Jesus wants to give His peace to our everyday life.

◆

D A Y   T W O

Peace and Activities

You can feel fulfilled by being involved in study programs in a wide variety of schools, colleges, institutes, and universities. You can feel challenged by the pursuit of a career or hobbies, learning a skill, becoming involved in a cause, attending an event, helping with charitable work, becoming involved in an exercise or weight-loss program or even working long and diligent hours in Christian work. Many activities can give satisfaction and pleasure to the participants without their giving God a thought.

Let's Go For It!

I met a prominent lawyer who was to introduce me as a banquet speaker. I asked him how he became a Christian.

He told me he was a star athlete and the top student in high school. When he received his diploma, he was disappointed. He thought there would be more satisfaction than he experienced. He entered Harvard College and received recognition and satisfaction from playing on the varsity football team. In the classroom he was a top student. But when he received his diploma he was disappointed not to experience satisfaction from this accomplishment. So he looked eagerly to law school at Yale, completing that program with top honors.

Once again, receiving his diploma left him with a vague feeling of emptiness and the thought that there must be more to life than this. When he received an invitation to join the prestigious law firm of his choice, his career was off to a good start. Then he and his wife designed and built their dream house. They looked forward to the day they would take possession; when that day came, there was no joy. There was an emptiness that career and marriage could not fill. "When that day came," he said, " we realized that there had to be more to life than this."

♦

Have you ever experienced the frustration of accomplishing something only to find out you were not satisfied?   Yes ❑   No ❑

Read Matthew 6:33. Where would you locate yourself between putting Christ's kingdom first versus where you currently give emphasis to activities?

_____

_____

He looked straight at me. "At that time I met a businessman with a serenity about him that caught my attention. In a conversation over lunch one day, I asked him why he seemed so content with life. He is the one who introduced me to the resources that are available to us from God. And that's why I am here to introduce you, Dr. Brandt."

The attorney found the flaw in depending on activities and events: they eventually come to an end and leave you empty.

Can you recall an event you eagerly looked forward to and left you disappointed when it was over?   Yes ❑   No ❑

Examine the Scriptures and/or your answers in today's lesson. Determine the most meaningful thought for you today. Write your thought for the day here:

_____

_____

_____

Applying what God is pointing out to you is essential. How will you apply this truth to your life today? _____

_____

Write a short prayer to God that summarizes your thoughts._____

_____

_____

_____

_____

Did God bring to mind someone who needs to hear this truth? Who?_____

_____

Thoughts for the Day:

A personal relationship with the Author of peace never ends.

———

Activities and events eventually come to an end and
leave you empty.

◆

D A Y   T H R E E

Peace and Things

It Will Make Me Happy!

This amazing world is filled with interesting things that can satisfy a restless heart and bring peace and contentment. We are all familiar with the calming effect of a pleasurable drive in a car. House furnishings, TVs, VCRs and stereos are pleasurable adult toys.

Most of us can recall happy moments enjoying a delicious meal together. Buying clothes, looking after the hair, the face, and the body are pleasant activities. The lawn, flowers, bushes, trees, and shrubs can provide hours of enjoyment and relaxation. Alcohol is the oil that eliminates social friction. Swallowing pills can calm you down or pick you up.

I was working overseas with a gentleman who was a highly successful and prominent engineer. He invited me to his home. His driveway was a quarter of a mile long; as we approached the house, I saw the six-car garage with a car in each one. The home had a butler, a chauffeur, a gardener, two maids, a nanny and a cook. The acreage was large and very private, with a horse stable, swimming pool, and tennis court. We had our own private accommodations in a separate wing of the house. He had everything money could buy, but his family was in shambles.

Read Matthew 19:16-22. The rich young ruler had everything money could buy. What was it that the rich young ruler could not buy?_____

_____

Is there something you once depended on for peace and discovered that it was not sufficient to bring peace after all? _____

_____

◆

At a family life conference where I had spoken during the previous year, he realized his life was empty and that during the accumulation of all his wealth he had neglected his wife and family. At the conference he had committed to establish a positive relationship with his family.

My purpose during this visit, a year after his first conference, was to see if I could help overcome some of the barriers that separated him from his wife and family. Sadly, as it turned out, his wife was not even willing to consider a closer relationship with him at this time. Here was the display of all the things money could buy. It was also a stark reminder that there are some things money cannot buy: the spirit of love, joy, peace and kindness flowing back and forth between parents, partners, and children. Today he remains committed to his goal with his family, but it may take a long time.

◆

Do you have a "thing" that comforts you? What is it?_____

_____

Examine the Scriptures and/or your answers in today's lesson. Determine the most meaningful thought for you today. Write your thought for the day here:

_____

_____

Applying what God is pointing out to you is essential. How will you apply this truth to your life today? _____

_____

Write a short prayer to God that summarizes your thoughts._____

_____

_____

_____

Did God bring to mind someone who needs to hear this truth? Who? _____

_____

Thought for the Day:

Things can be bought with money and bring counterfeit peace. Lasting peace can only come with a relationship to Jesus Christ.

◆

D A Y   F O U R

Peace and People

Can Anything Beat Friendship?

Greater love has no one than this, that one lay down his life for his friends. You are my friends if you do what I command.
JOHN 15:13–14, NIV

An obvious pathway to find relief from tension and stress is to pour out our thoughts and feelings to a sympathetic listener. I've spent most of my life as a counselor, and I can assure you that you can find relief through counseling and therapy without giving God a thought.

A newspaper report on a conference of survivors of suicides featured one mother's story. Her world ended on the day her son killed himself. She told other survivors of suicides that their feelings of anguish, anger, and guilt are normal. Eventually she allowed her feelings of guilt to wash away when her therapist helped her realize she wasn't to blame.[1]

One human being helping another: a pat on the back, a friendly hug, or a compliment from someone you care about is delightfully soothing.

The sympathy and affection that self-help groups give each other is often the only source of help that keeps many a weary soul from giving up. Every Monday, a list of dozens of support groups appears in our local paper. Table 1 below lists some of the groups.

A pleasing sense of belonging and approval comes as a part of a cooperative effort, such as playing on a team, sharing a work project, sensing the appreciative response of others in the use of your talents.

And what can be more satisfying than for a young man and a young lady to meet and experience an irresistible attraction toward one another that deepens into a satisfying relationship? Finally these two, usually opposites, gradually blend their lives into a partnership.

Table 1: Support Groups	
Mended Hearts, Inc.	Smokers Anonymous
Alcoholics Anonymous	Food Addicts Anonymous
Bereavement Support Group	People Who Love Too Much
Compassionate Friends	Narcotics Anonymous
Emotions Anonymous	Family, Friends, and Lovers (AIDS)
Women Who Love Too Much	Take Off Pounds Sensibly
Arthritis Foundation	Co-Dependents in Relationships
Living with Breast Cancer	Adult Children of Alcoholics
Caregivers Support Group	Rebuilders (divorced & separated)
Overeaters Anonymous	Children with Learning Disabilities
Coping with Cancer	Alliance for the Mentally Ill
Miscarriage Support Group	Hospice Bereavement Support Group
Alzheimer's Support Group	Impaired Nurses Support Group
M.A.D.D	Support Group for Interfaith Couples
Nursing Home Support Group	C.A.R.P Parent Support Group (Families affected by drug and alcohol abuse)

There is just something special and satisfying about a deepening friendship between two people, male or female, which contains the unmistakable comfort of heart-to-heart talks. Teaching, learning and serving also give you a sense of accomplishment that is deeply satisfying.

◆

Can you think of a person who is a calming influence on your life? _____

_____

◆

Examine the Scriptures and/or your answers in today's lesson. Determine the most meaningful thought for you today. Write your thought for the day here:

_____

_____

_____

_____

Applying what God is pointing out to you is essential. How will you apply this truth to your life today? _____

_____

_____

Write a short prayer to God that summarizes your thoughts. _____

_____

_____

_____

_____

Did God bring to mind someone who needs to hear this truth? Who? _____

_____

Thought for the Day:
Friendship is unstable and unpredictable. Jesus is the same yesterday, today, and forever.

◆

DAY FIVE

Peace and Jesus

Why Doesn't It Work? The Rest of the Story!

I have attempted to create a picture of the finest and best features in this wonderful world. The humanist is right: This world contains ample resources that, coupled with the best efforts of caring people, should result in a world full of satisfied, happy people. But, alas, there is a flaw in this beautiful picture.

You would think you could find continuous satisfaction, peace and enjoyment from family life, social life, friendships, school and church associates, and professional contacts without giving God a thought.

As I reflect across the last decade, the death of my wife Eva interrupted that human fellowship. I married again and three years later my wife Marcey died suddenly. Jim Baker, one of my best friends who traveled with me all over the world, suddenly died of a brain aneurysm; He was only fifty-two. Art DeMoss, a fifty-three-year-old businessman with whom I shared ministry assignments many times, died of a heart attack on the tennis court. A college official whom I respected greatly suddenly announced he was resigning his position, divorcing his wife, and marrying someone else. Just several weeks ago, a tearful young lady with two young children told me that her husband had announced he was leaving her. No warning. No explanation.

Time, on September 15, 1986, reported that the health cost of drug abuse was estimated by one National Center for Health statistics study at $59.7 billion. The medical bill for alcohol abuse was estimated at an astonishing $146.7 billion.

Earlier in this chapter, I wrote optimistically about the pleasures of courtship that deepens into a happy, lifetime marriage. Present reality shatters that beautiful hope. During the first quarter of 1991 there were 413,000 marriages and 285,000 divorces.

I wrote of the benefits of friendship, cooperation, teamwork, and recognition. To my dismay, I listen to a daily recital of the failure of human effort, of marriage partners who have deceived and cheated each other. We have become accustomed to reports of lying, cheating, and stealing in business and politics. There is strife and discord at every level of life: from the boardroom to the classroom to the family room.

The Florida legislature is currently struggling with what to do to halt teenage pregnancy. About twenty-five thousand teenagers gave birth last year in Florida, costing more than $125 million in subsidized health care and welfare payments. More than one million teenagers became pregnant last year in our country, and almost half chose to have abortions. Ninety-two percent of these pregnancies were unintended.

In this wonderful world, families are breaking up, incidents of child abuse and other family violence are growing, and delinquency, theft, murder and crime, escalating venereal diseases, and emotional disorders threaten our survival. There are multitudes starving to death and nations are destroying each other.

Finding relief from tension is what some may think of as peace. People often turn to friendship, fellowship, challenges, opportunities, travel, and materialism, but they are as illusive as turning to drugs and alcohol. Initially there is hope, comfort, pleasure, but sooner or later our efforts turn to ashes and result in increased loneliness, grief, tension, or bitterness.

The *Human Manifesto II* says: "Happiness and the creative realization of human needs and desires, individually and in shared enjoyment, are continuous themes of humanism. Critical intelligence, infused by a sense of human caring, is the best method that humanity has for resolving problems." (p.18)

It seems clear to me that the finest human effort in a magnificent world is not enough to quiet the human heart in times of trouble and stress.

Jesus said: "These things I have spoken to you, that in Me you may have peace. In the world you will have tribulation; but be of good cheer, I have overcome the world." (JOHN 16:33, NKJV)

♦

What does this verse mean to you? Try to write in your own words how this verse can help you today. _____

_____

_____

_____

_____

◆

Can you recall a heart-to-heart talk that relieved some of your tensions? _____

_____

_____

    Based on all the options we have in going after peace, we should take careful note when Jesus gently tells us to turn to Him for peace. We can turn to Him, and not the world, if the peace we seek is to be deeply satisfying and lasting.

◆

Examine the Scriptures and/or your answers in today's lesson. Determine the most meaningful thought for you today. Write your thought for the day here:

_____

_____

_____

_____

Applying what God is pointing out to you is essential. How will you apply this truth to your life today? _____

_____

_____

Write a short prayer to God that summarizes your thoughts. _____

_____

_____

_____

Did God bring to mind someone who needs to hear this truth? Who? _____

_____

Thought for the Day:

The finest human effort in a magnificent world is not enough to quiet the human heart in times of trouble and stress.

◆

(Optional—But Recommended!)

Bring forward your thoughts from each day:

1. _____
2. _____
3. _____
4. _____
5. _____

Bring forward your application:

1. _____
2. _____
3. _____
4. _____
5. _____
6. _____

Bring forward your prayers:

1. _____
2. _____
3. _____
4. _____
5. _____
6. _____

Bring forward who you shared your thoughts with:

1. _____
2. _____
3. _____
4. _____
5. _____
6. _____

Thought for the Week:

As long as you are busy, you may not notice a lack of peace.
When you slow down, it can become a glaring reality.

◆

UNIT THREE

Most of Us Had a Poor Start in Life!

Thought Starter:

Why do people blame their present behavior on their
past experiences?

♦

Memory Verse for the Week:

See to it that no one takes you captive through hollow and deceptive philosophy, which depends on human tradition and the basic principles of
this world rather than on Christ.

COLOSSIANS 2:8, NIV

DAY ONE

Beware lest anyone cheat you through philosophy and empty deceit,
according to the tradition of men, according to the basic principles of the
world, and not according to Christ. For in Him dwells all the
fullness of the Godhead bodily; and you are complete in Him,
who is the head of all principality and power.
COLOSSIANS 2:8–10, NKJV

Real Life

Malcom and Dorothy sit, stone faced, across from the counselor in the consulting room with an invisible wall between them. They are very busy Christians who have been married for twenty-two miserable years.

She says that he does not treat her like a doormat, but like the dirt under a doormat! She would do anything in the world for him, she says: "If only he would show some appreciation and give me just a little bit of affection and tenderness. But no, he just takes me for granted. All he wants is for me to wash his clothes, cook his meals and keep the house. He is a very proud, selfish, bad-tempered man, given to very loud yelling."

Suppose these two were some of your closest friends, how would you try to help them? _____

_____

_____

To show how inconsiderate he is, she told how he bought her the Lincoln she drives when he knew perfectly well that she wanted a Cadillac. She must even beg him for a meager allowance. But today, the counselor looks at a well-groomed, elegantly dressed lady and observes that underneath the expensive clothing is a very hostile, bitter woman.

They live in a large, professionally decorated, color coordinated, beautifully furnished and landscaped house. They could not wish for a better air-conditioned place in which to carry on their bitter relationship. Their two children live on the opposite side of the country, as far away from their parents as they could get. The maid does her best to avoid getting chewed out by either one of them.

Malcom sits there shaking his head, teeth clenched, as he listens to her side of the story. When it is his turn he describes her as a spoiled, selfish, demanding person. From the start of their marriage everything had to go her way, from keeping the house, to when they ate, choosing friends and activities, raising the children, choosing their clothes, and on and on. He finally gave up on her and concentrated on developing his business. He let her run the house and the family. He had his territory; she had hers. Their buffer zone was the children. Now the children are gone and all that is left between them is mutual hostility and strong differences of opinion.

Malcom had been raised in a lower class European family where the father called all the shots and the women followed instructions. His father had a violent temper and would abuse the family verbally and sometimes physically. Malcom is much like his father, except he never physically abused anyone. He admits to being self-centered.

Dorothy grew up in an upper middle-class home. She had very few limits, was quite self-centered, and often pouted when she couldn't have her way. She could be called a spoiled child. Her parents provided a stable home and her mother tended to dominate the family.

Obviously there is more to each of their histories. But at this point she will only admit to being a misunderstood lady and this brings great frustration to her.

When this couple began to seek help, they could have turned to a counselor with either a humanist or a biblical perspective. The two approaches would be quite different.

The study of how humans affect or help one another is humanism.

How would you define humanism? _____

_____

_____

Webster's dictionary defines humanism as: "A doctrine, set of attitudes, a way of life centered upon human interests or values; a philosophy that rejects supernaturalism, regards man as a natural object, and asserts the essential dignity and worth of man and his capacity to achieve self-realization through the use of reason and scientific method."

Although the name is current, humanism, as a philosophy of life, is nothing new. Rejecting God and centering a way of life and a way of thinking around man's interests and values has been around since the beginning of time.

Recall an instance when you were helped by a person. _____

_____

Examine the *Scriptures* and/or your answers in today's lesson. Determine the most meaningful thought for you today. Write your thought for the day here:

_____

_____

_____

Applying what God is pointing out to you is essential. How will you apply this truth to your life today? _____

_____

Write a short prayer to God that summarizes your thoughts._____

_____

_____

_____

Did God bring to mind someone who needs to hear this truth? Who? _____

_____

Thought for the Day:

Real life always needs a supernatural perspective
if we are to gain real help.

◆

DAY TWO

Blame Your Background

In graduate school my professors identified a rather predictable response caused by growing up in a restrictive environment. They identified a poor start in life as one that hinders self-expression, frustrates pleasure needs, and provides wrong reinforcers.

They taught that the consequences of growing up in this type of environment are adults who will respond to the circumstances of life with the following ways:

Responses that Humanists Believe Are Caused by Our Environment		
Hostility	Resentment	Hate
Pessimism	Fear	Doubt
Perplexity	In Conflict	Confusion
Pain	Depression	Indifference
Cruelty	Lack of generosity	Rage
Oppression of others		

Time magazine featured an article entitled, "The Burnout of Almost Everyone": "They describe the stages of burnout, progressing from intense enthusiasm and job satisfaction, to exhaustion, physical illness, acute anger and depression. Even the best worker, when thwarted, will swallow his rage; it then turns into a small private conflagration, an internal fire in his engine room."[1]

According to these authors, the consequence to adults of being thwarted (i.e., not getting their own way) by other adults (i.e., husbands and wives) are *rage and hostility,* resulting in physical illness, depression, and tension headaches.

No doubt people who struggle with the responses listed above do come from faulty family backgrounds, unloving relationships, difficult experiences, and situations in which there was little opportunity given to express themselves.

Furthermore, given proper alteration in the people, circumstances, and social conditions that surround an individual, changes can occur without giving God a thought. Or counseling, done by trained, caring, kindly people, and followed up by appropriate changes, can bring great relief to an anxious, confused person. If you want relief, you can find it in this wonderful world. Who needs God?

A change of location or the removal of a troublesome person can give relief to an anxious person. That is relief, not healing. Alcohol can quiet a hostile, bitter heart, but it only gives relief, not healing.

Check the following items that can give you relief but not healing:

♦ A change in your location.
♦ Time.
♦ Finding a new circle of friends.
♦ A change in your heart.
♦ A new job.

If the couple we described at the beginning of this chapter would turn to a humanist counselor for help, the counselor would develop a detailed study of their backgrounds, their stormy marriage, and their response to each other at present. From this information, the counselor would help them understand how their backgrounds have shaped their outlook on life, what their needs are, what ways they are frustrating each other's needs, and what adjustments can be made in order to satisfy each other's needs.

Describe an experience of calming down when a certain person left. _____

_____

_____

Examine the Scriptures and/or your answers in today's lesson. Determine the most meaningful thought for you today. Write your thought for the day here:

_____

_____

_____

Applying what God is pointing out to you is essential. How will you apply this truth to your life today? _____

_____

_____

Write a short prayer to God that summarizes your thoughts. _____

_____

_____

_____

_____

Did God bring to mind someone who needs to hear this truth? Who?_____

_____

Thought for the Day:

Changes in your environment will not bring healing to your heart.

◆

DAY THREE

Understand Relief
Versus Healing

Hopefully, as Dorothy gains some understanding of both her needs and Malcom's, and senses that he is making adjustments with her needs in mind, her anger and bitterness will be calmed and she will experience some peace of mind, become more hopeful, more affectionate, and more desirous of meeting his needs.

Do you believe that most people try to correct their life by changing their circumstances? Why? _____

_____

_____

As Malcom gains some understanding of his and Dorothy's needs, makes some adjustments on her behalf, and senses that she is seeking to meet his needs, his quarrelsomeness and hot temper will cool. They can then develop a friendship and discover the joy of living as he works to meet her needs.

Just imagine how relieved these people would be if the counselor could help them in this way.

I emphasize that they can find blessed relief by following this approach, but not a change of heart.

What causes change as a result of relief? We could compare this change to the relief experienced if you take a pain pill. Change happens swiftly. You get relief but not healing. Isn't it good to get relief? Of course, as long as you don't kid yourself and you understand it is relief and not healing.

Recently, I learned a lesson about the quick, comforting effect of drugs. I had a tooth pulled and it developed what my dentist called a "dry socket." My jaw became infected and it spread to the side of my face so that at any one moment I experienced incredible, unbearable pain around my eye, ear, sinuses, jaw and throat. The pain was so intense I was ready to do anything for some relief!

Isn't it good to get relief? _____

Is there something better than relief? _____

My dentist handed me an envelope containing some little pills. After swallowing one, the pain gradually disappeared. To maintain freedom from pain, all I had to do was keep swallowing those pills.

Everyone knows that pain pills do not cure the source of the pain. Healing must also happen. So I knew that the condition of my jaw had not changed. But that didn't matter. I would have paid *any* price for those pills. (This incident was a clear lesson to me of how easily anyone can become dependent on pills for a sense of well-being.) Having one's needs met, similarly, brings relief, not healing.

Our couple could seek out a Christian who is trained in humanistic counseling, who would proceed in the same methods as the humanistic counselor. They could seek out a biblical counselor, who would also recognize that the woman's anger, her bitter response to her husband, and his quarrelsomeness and nasty temper were barriers to a healthy marriage. The humanist would say these responses are socially caused. The Bible-based counselor would call them sin.

A very, very, very important decision: By faith the humanist says that anger, bitterness, quarrelsomeness, or a nasty temper is caused by the way you have been treated; by faith, the biblical counselor says that these characteristics are caused by sin; by faith, what do you say? Your decision will determine where you turn for help!

If both approaches bring relief, what does it matter which approach you use?

_____

_____

If you fail to deal with the sin, the relief you experience is like taking a pain pill for a toothache without fixing the tooth.

Think of a situation in which you found relief. How did you get relief? _____

_____

Examine the Scriptures and/or your answers in today's lesson. Determine the most meaningful thought for you today. Write your thought for the day here:

_____

_____

_____

Applying what God is pointing out to you is essential. How will you apply this truth to your life today? _____

_____

Write a short prayer to God that summarizes your thoughts._____

_____

_____

_____

Did God bring to mind someone who needs to hear this truth? Who?_____

_____

Thought for the Day:

Relief is good, but remember, it is not healing.

◆

D A Y   F O U R

Blame Your Sin

Finding relief from sin instead of obtaining cleansing is a cruel trap. Like my situation with the pain pill, I am comfortably sick. Relief from sin allows me to be comfortably separated from God.

A follower of Jesus takes the subject of sin seriously. We do indeed face very serious social problems. If it is sin that is the cause, there couldn't be any better news: *There is a cure for sin.*

Review these thoughts before you proceed: (1) There is no human remedy for sin. (2) If it is sin, that's good news. It is the simplest thing in the world to deal with. Jesus died to cleanse us from sin.

Many years ago, I contracted malaria. I alternately perspired and shivered, my joints ached, and I struggled with a high fever. One of the missionaries said, "It's only malaria. Take these pills and go to bed. Tomorrow you will be better." Sure enough, it worked.

Several years later my wife and her friend, who traveled with us in a part of Africa, became very ill after we returned home to the United States. They had the same malaria symptoms that I had previously, and they tried to tell their doctor what it was. He wouldn't listen, hospitalized them, and subjected them to a variety of tests and x-rays. In the meantime they both suffered with high fever, chills and pain. Three days later the doctor consulted a tropical medicine specialist who diagnosed malaria. He prescribed the same pills I had taken and in one day they were better. They went through five days of unnecessary suffering because the doctor didn't know what to treat.

Dealing with sin is like that. The cure is swift and sure if you use the proper diagnosis and proper treatment. You can suffer greatly from the ravages of sin while you are sincerely and carefully trying to correct the suffering by following the wrong diagnosis and the wrong treatment.

Are you suffering from the ravages of sin while you are sincerely and carefully trying to correct the problem? Maybe you are using the wrong treatment. Take a few moments and ask God if there is a besetting sin that you need to deal with. Allow the Holy Spirit to deal with your heart concerning the issue.

In the case of my wife and her friend, the doctor had never seen malaria and therefore tried to find a cause familiar to him.

The same can happen when one deals with symptoms the Bible calls sin. There is no debate about the symptoms; everyone agrees on what they are. What is debatable is the cause.

The Bible says contention and outbursts of anger are works of the flesh or sin. If one or both people in a disagreement accept this diagnosis, they will turn God-ward, confess their sins, repent, and receive forgiveness, cleansing, and renewal.

If they reject the diagnosis as sin and believe the very same symptoms are socially or culturally caused, they will proceed to investigate exposure to family, friends, church, community, etc., for an explanation.

Dr. S. I. McMillen, a long-time friend of mine, spent many years studying the biblical principles and directions on living in Jewish and Christian writings. As a result of this research he wrote a best-seller called *None of These Diseases,* which describes the physical consequences of wrong living. He pointed out that there may be sin in the picture when aches and pains show up:

Peace does not come in capsules! This is regrettable because medical science recognizes that emotions such as fear, sorrow, envy, resentment and hatred are responsible for the majority of our sicknesses. Estimates vary from 60 percent to nearly 100 percent. Emotional stress can cause high blood pressure, toxic goiter, migraine headaches, arthritis, apoplexy, heart trouble, gastrointestinal ulcers, and other serious diseases too numerous to mention. As physicians we can prescribe medicine for the symptoms of these diseases, but we can not do much for the underlying cause, emotional turmoil. It is lamentable that peace does not come in capsules. We need something more than a pill for the disease-producing stresses of the man who has lost his life's savings, the tearful feminine soul who has been jilted, the young father who has an inoperable cancer, the woman whose husband is a philanderer, the distraught teenager with a facial birthmark, and the schemer who lies awake at night trying to think of ways to get even with his neighbor . . . No one can appreciate so fully as a doctor the amazingly large percentage of human disease and suffering which is directly traceable to worry, fear, conflict, immorality, dissipation, and ignorance, to unwholesome thinking and unclean living. The sincere acceptance of the principles and teachings of Christ with respect to the life of mental peace and joy, the life of unselfish thought and clean living, would at once wipe out more than half the difficulties, diseases, and sorrows of the human race.[2]

A Christian with a biblical perspective and a Christian with a humanistic perspective can both be sincere, committed people who are looking at the same situation, but they will come up with different causes and different solutions.

Alexander Pope described how sin captures us:
> *Vice is a monster of so frightful mien,*
> *As to be hated needs but to be seen;*
> *Yet seen too oft, familiar with her face,*
> *We first endure, then pity, then embrace.*

Humanistic thinking can be like that. First, we study it in order to understand it. Then we shake our heads in disagreement, then listen some more to be sure we heard correctly, and finally, unknowingly, begin to absorb it.

If you are dealing with sin, you must turn to the Creator and Savior for cleansing, strengthening, and changing. If it is sin, society didn't put it into you; society only stirs up what is already in you. If it is sin, society can't help you. It requires a supernatural cure.

If you want relief, you can find it in this world. If you want a cure, only God can help you. As Tournier says, there is no human cure for sin.

Think of an experience when you were aware of sin and were cured. Write your results here: _____

_____

Examine the Scriptures and/or your answers in today's lesson. Determine the most meaningful thought for you today. Write your thought for the day here:

_____

_____

_____

_____

Applying what God is pointing out to you is essential. How will you apply this truth to your life today? _____

_____

Write a short prayer to God that summarizes your thoughts._____

_____

_____

_____

_____

Did God bring to mind someone who needs to hear this truth? Who?_____

_____

Thoughts for the Day:

There is a cure for sin!

————

The cure is swift and sure if you use the proper diagnosis and proper treatment.

◆

DAY FIVE

The Miracle of a
Cleansed Life

The couple in this lesson became my clients. They had been to three counselors before coming to "last-resort Brandt." One counselor was a humanist and not a Christian and the other two were "Christian humanists." The counselors had actually worked with the couple individually and had gone into a detailed study of both their backgrounds, reviewing their twenty-year history of antagonism and discord. The couple came away from the counselors with the verdict that they had irreconcilable differences and divorce was the only solution.

But during the time with each previous counselor, the woman had come away from each session greatly relieved. She was appreciative of their understanding, kindness, and willingness to listen to her. She felt that they understood that she was ready to change, but that her husband wouldn't cooperate. She felt that the counselors understood why she was bitter and hostile under the circumstances with which she had to live.

The husband was very disgusted with the whole process. He tolerated going only for the sake of the marriage. In his opinion, they just sided with her and did not really grasp what a problem she had created for him in their marriage. So, as a result, she was helped in finding great relief for herself, but the marriage was actually worse.

It was immediately evident to me that she had two problems: first, a personal problem of sin in the areas of anger and bitterness, and second, the marriage.

He had two problems also: first, the personal problem of sin in the areas of quarrelsomeness and a nasty temper, and second, the marriage.

They turned to God for their solution and in six weeks they were behaving like honeymooners! Interestingly, I never did talk to them about their marriage.

I am not trying to say that their marriage problems evaporated. What I am saying is that they now approached their problems without hostility, quarreling, and yelling as they allowed the Lord to give them peaceful, loving and joyful hearts. At that point they didn't need me and were quite capable of approaching their marriage problems in a friendly fashion and to begin to solve them.

This is the Christian miracle of the cleansed life—a great mystery—why after years of fighting would Malcolm and Dorothy submit to these biblical guidelines?

> You must rid yourselves of all such things as these: anger, rage, malice, slander, and filthy language from your lips (Col. 3:8).

> Clothe yourselves with compassion, kindness, humility, gentleness, and patience (Col. 3:12).

Examine yourself. Are you a Christian who turns to God for help? Are you a Christian and a partial humanist who turns to the environment for relief from sin? Are you a humanist who accepts scientific investigation only and rejects the biblical record?

Has the Bible ever come alive in your life? Explain: _____

_____

_____

_____

Here is His promise: "For I know the plans I have for you, declares the Lord, 'plans to prosper you and not to harm you, plans to give you hope and a future. Then you will call upon me and come and pray to me, and I will listen to you. You will seek me and find me when you seek me with all your heart'" (Jer. 29:11–13, NIV).

Examine the Scriptures and/or your answers in today's lesson. Determine the most meaningful thought for you today. Write your thought for the day here.

_____

_____

_____

Applying what God is pointing out to you is essential. How will you apply this truth to your life today? _____

_____

Write a short prayer to God that summarizes your thoughts._____

_____

_____

_____

_____

Did God bring to mind someone who needs to hear this truth? Who?_____

_____

Thought for the Day:

A cleansed life allows you to look at life from the proper perspective.

◆

(Optional—But Recommended!)

Bring forward your thoughts from each day:

1. _____
2. _____
3. _____
4. _____
5. _____

Bring forward your application:

1. _____
2. _____
3. _____
4. _____
5. _____

Bring forward your prayers:

1. _____
2. _____
3. _____
4. _____
5. _____

Bring forward who you shared your thoughts with:

1. _____

2. _____

3. _____

4. _____

5. _____

Thought for the Week:

My environment can give me relief from sin; only the Lord
can cure it.

◆

UNIT FOUR

God's Sharpest Tools; My Biggest Problems

Thought Starter:

Can you explain the change in some people's lives when they became Christians?

◆

Memory Verse for the Week:

Now if I am doing what I don't want to, it is plain where the trouble is: sin still has me in its evil grasp.
Romans 7:20, TLB

DAY ONE

"Men can only reproduce human life, but the Holy Spirit gives new life from heaven; so don't be surprised at my statement that you must be born again!"
JOHN 3:6–7, TLB

Born Again

I have spent over forty years counseling people from a biblical perspective. I work with disturbed people. My first serious encounter with a disturbed person was with myself.

Have you ever come to the conclusion that you are a disturbed person?

_____

What helped you to realize this?_____

_____

I grew up in a church environment. During my late teens, I said to myself, "I don't need a bunch of rules to run my life, let alone a bunch of rules that keep me from having fun!"

I had some friends who taught me how much fun I could have with alcohol. I hit the bars, the parties, the streets and the homes of my friends (when the parents were gone!). Mixed in with all this was considerable girl-chasing. My mission in life was to entice "religious" young people away from church and into the "good life." I had been successful with my share of converts at the bar. Those were wonderful fun-filled years, but such a life was also the broad road to destruction.

My way of life came to an abrupt halt. Three of my drinking buddies burned to death in a fiery head-on collision. One of my friends, a brilliant young lady, committed suicide. The heavy-drinking, kindly man who ran the pool room, one of my local hang-outs, slammed his car into a telephone pole one night and was killed instantly. Lastly, I was fired from my job because I returned from lunch drunk one day.

Right after all this happened, Bill, one of my best friends and the heaviest drinker of all, suddenly announced that he had become a Christian. He had wandered into a Christian meeting by accident and stayed to hear the speaker. God's Holy Spirit touched his heart. He went forward at the end of the meeting and publicly invited Christ to take over his life and heart and to deal with his sin. He told me later, "I felt like I was the only guy the speaker was talking to!"

Virtually overnight Bill demonstrated that he was finished with my kind of life. He went to church twice on Sunday and every Wednesday. He dated only "Christian" girls. He limited his activities to swimming, hiking, tennis, ice-skating, and skiing. In order to continue my friendship with him, I was forced to accept his way of life.

For a few months I lived on both sides of the fence. Bill and I had long arguments about his faith and his changed life. I argued fervently on behalf of the old way of life, the rollicking nights, the warmth of kindred spirits and good fellowship in our favorite bars! I could just as well have been talking to the wall. Bill's change wasn't temporary. He turned a deaf ear to my fervent, earnest efforts to save him from a restrictive, limited, narrow life.

Take a few minutes to reflect back over your personal salvation testimony. The Christian's life is strengthened when he/she remembers their salvation experience. What was your life like before you accepted Christ? _____

_____

_____

_____

How did you realize God was speaking to you? _____

_____

_____

_____

How did you become a Christian? _____

_____

_____

_____

How did Christ affect your life? _____

_____

_____

_____

One afternoon I staggered home drunk and dropped off to sleep on a couch. A Christian businessman, who had come to sell my mother a stove, shook me awake. He read me a simple tract about receiving Christ. I had heard this familiar old story all my life. He asked me to pray with him, and in a drunken stupor, I asked the Lord to come into my heart. I then rolled over and went back to sleep!

Later in the evening, when I awoke, I didn't remember the encounter with the stove man and I was not aware of any change. My only thought was to return to my favorite bar; however, that night the people around the bar seemed to be babbling, slurring their words, and talking foolishly. The bartender was carelessly sloshing the glasses in dirty water. The room was smoke-filled and unbearably noisy. I didn't have fun that night.

I found myself at the beginning of the end of my drinking days. In a matter of weeks, I longed for Bill's way of life. The old way simply died away. I didn't even remember the encounter with the stove salesman until I began looking back later on my changed behavior.

What followed in my life proved to me with abundant clarity that God will answer a sincere call for help, even if the prayer is mumbled by someone who drinks too much, who slurs his words, and whose memory is blurred. Looking back on that event years ago, all I can remember of the discussion with the man in our living room is that what he said seemed to make sense.

I have a Ph.D. in marriage and the family and have spent my life studying, teaching, and counseling in the area of Christian living. Today, forty years later, I still cannot totally explain what happened to me when I was "born again," or even why it happened to me. When Nicodemus, one of the smartest and most educated men of his day, asked Jesus, "What in the world are you talking about when you say, 'born again'?" Jesus replied:

> "What I am telling you so earnestly is this: Unless one is born of water and the Spirit, he cannot enter the Kingdom of God. Men can only reproduce human life, but the Holy Spirit gives new life from heaven; so don't be surprised at my statement that you must be born again! Just as you can hear the wind but can't tell where it comes from or where it will go next, so it is with the Spirit. We do not know on whom he will next bestow this life from heaven."
>
> JOHN 3:5–8, TLB

Examine the Scriptures and/or your answers in today's lesson. Determine the most meaningful thought for you today. Write your thought for the day here:

_____

_____

_____

_____

Applying what God is pointing out to you is essential. How will you apply this truth to your life today? _____

_____

Write a short prayer to God that summarizes your thoughts._____

_____

_____

_____

Did God bring to mind someone who needs to hear this truth? Who?

_____

Thought for the Day:

"Born again" can only be understood if you are born again.

♦

D A Y   T W O

Sin's Grasp

Swearing, drinking, and antagonism toward the church dropped away like dead leaves, but over a period of several years my sense of closeness to the Lord began to fade. Marriage, parenthood, and job revealed deeper life problems of anger, bitterness, hostility and pride.

My boss was a harsh, cussing man. Day after day he would scowl as he scanned the engineering department from his glass-walled office. Stuffing his mouth with a huge chunk of tobacco, he would yell, "Brandt!" And that was all it took! Anger would well up within me and I was a goner! It worked every time; I was helpless. Even before his merciless tongue-lashings, I would be brimming with hostility and wounded pride.

How could I vent my feelings toward him? I would have found myself out in the street! As a result of keeping my anger inside, it spilled over into my relationships with my wife, my son, and my associates. I was filled with regret over the things I said and did. Telling myself to stop didn't help. I tried everything I could to find relief: taking a walk, griping to a friend, playing tennis, yelling at my wife or tiny son. *I even consciously thought about swearing and drinking again!* Typical regressive behavior. I even tried looking into my neglected Bible.

Is there a person, place, thing, or event that affects you like this? _____

_____

What is your solution? _____

_____

_____

I quickly found out that Bible reading was not easy. I couldn't scan the Bible and ignore parts of it like reading a newspaper. What I read was disturbing, but some of it slipped into my mind and I found myself comparing my behavior to the verses that I read.

I came upon a verse that got my attention: "Stop being mean, bad-tempered and angry. Quarreling, harsh words, and dislike of others have no place in your lives. Instead, be kind to each other, tenderhearted, forgiving one another, just as God has forgiven you because you belong to Christ" (Eph. 4:31–32, TLB).

How does this Scripture passage speak to you today? Please write your response. _____

_____

_____

I spent several months contemplating those verses. They made me mad! The more I thought about forgiving my boss, my family and my associates, the more reasons I found for *not* forgiving them. I easily justified my hatred and anger. Why should I be kind and tenderhearted toward them? Such an idea infuriated me!

Eventually I came to the conclusion that the Bible was right. I told myself, "I will quit being hateful and angry toward these people." But as the days passed, I made a scary and frustrating discovery: I couldn't quit! When my boss yelled at me or my wife didn't do what I asked her to do, my response was automatic: intense anger! I could cover it up, put a smile on my face and control my speech, but just underneath the surface was a furious response.

My resentment toward the Bible intensified. Here was a book that required something that I didn't want to do and couldn't do *even after I decided to do it!*

Does this ever happen to you? _____

We tend to resist the Bible if we are not living according to it!

I identified with the apostle Paul when he described himself: "When I want to do good, I don't; and when I try not to do wrong, I do it anyway. Now if I am doing what I don't want to, it is plain where the trouble is: sin still has me in its evil grasp" (Rom. 7:19–20, TLB).

As I continued to thumb through my Bible, I stumbled upon some verses which hit me right between the eyes: "Not that we are in any way confident of our own resources—our ability comes from God. It is he who makes us competent administrators of the new agreement, and we deal not in the letter but in the Spirit. The letter of the Law leads to the death of the soul; the Spirit alone can give life to the soul" (2 Cor. 3:5–6, PHILLIPS).

Has this lesson pointed out any sin? _____

_____

Examine the Scriptures and/or your answers in today's lesson. Determine the most meaningful thought for you today. Write your thought for the day here:

_____

_____

_____

Applying what God is pointing out to you is essential. How will you apply this truth to your life today? _____

_____

_____

Write a short prayer to God that summarizes your thoughts. _____

_____

_____

_____

Did God bring to mind someone who needs to hear this truth? Who?_____

_____

Thought for the Day:

The Word of God speaks to your problem quicker and deeper than any human personality.

♦

DAY THREE

Your Resources Are Not Enough

My response to those verses was troubled. Why couldn't I depend upon my own resources for living? *I* earned an education without God's help. *I* obtained a job and promotions. By my own will *I* managed to meet the demands of life. It appeared to me that *I* could do some things *on my own!*

After a long struggle I realized that what *I could not do* is live up to the *spirit* of Christianity. I could live up to "the letter" by acting kind, tenderhearted and forgiving. But I found that *acting* killed something in me; it was death to my soul. The Christian life was not the development of my acting ability! The Christian life was God's Spirit living His life in me.

Examine yourself today. Write in your own words anything in your Christian life that is just an act._____

_____

_____

Is there something in your life that you wouldn't want to write? _____

_____

Why is it in your life? _____

_____

_____

How are you going to deal with it?_____

_____

_____

After admitting that my own resources were not enough, I faced other spiritual obstacles: Why did my fellowship with Jesus fade after my conversion? Why did God seem so distant, so unconcerned? Worst of all, why did God sometimes seem not to exist at all?

The Bible met all my questions with a single answer: "Listen now! The Lord isn't too weak to save you. And He isn't getting deaf! He can hear when you call! But the trouble is that your sins have cut you off from God. Because of sin He has turned His face away from you and will not listen anymore" (Isa. 59:1–2, TLB).

The Bible put the finger on the problem: sin was keeping me at a distance from the Lord. Those verses that disturbed me said it all: "Stop being mean, bad tempered, and angry . . . harsh words and dislike of others should have no place in your lives" (Eph. 4:31, TLB).

These were the sins that made God seem so distant to me. My boss and family didn't cause them; they were only used to reveal them in me.

Does sin disturb you? If so, explain how it disturbs you. _____

_____

_____

_____

Since only God could cleanse me from sin, I asked Him to cleanse my heart. I also asked the Lord for help because I knew I couldn't help myself. I couldn't love my boss or my wife or my little boy. Oh, yes, I could *seem* loving, but that's not the same as *being* loving on the inside. The turning point came when I admitted to God that I was helpless and asked Him to give me His love for my boss *when he was yelling at me.* The next day on the way to work I again appealed to God to take away the intense anger when my boss yelled at me and give me His love for my boss.

I remember very well the day when my boss, his jaw loaded with tobacco, shouted, "Brandt!" and to my surprise, I wasn't mad at him. For the first time that I could remember, the smile on my face reflected my spirit. What an incredible experience for me! I'm not trying to say that I entrusted every day to the Lord. But every day that I did, I found the Lord was always there.

A few weeks later, my boss yelled at me again: "Brandt! Come in here!" By now he amused me. I actually enjoyed watching him! Let me tell you! What a different experience it was when there was joy in my heart! I could watch an old crab and not become a crab myself! It was wonderful to be released from that trap. I walked into his office feeling friendly and relaxed. I asked, "What do you want?" And he said, "What's gotten into you? You've been in a good mood lately!"

As the days went by my boss still yelled, but I was not mad at him. It was a miracle. First came cleansing; then came strength: a strength not my own but God's.

I cannot change what I am down deep inside: only God can. I can only change surface actions. I have a human tendency to idealistically view myself: I think I can change my behavior if I am just determined enough. This thinking leads to some great acting, but not to a changed and *cured* heart. I may feel that I must add to the finished work of Christ, but when Jesus said, "It is finished" (John 19:30, NKJV). He meant it.

Only Jesus lived the Christian life. Only Jesus, in control of our hearts, will enable us to live the Christian life today. Every day that I yielded to Him, I found the Lord was always there. And across these years, the principle that we can live the Christian life with God in control and win against sin has made a tremendous difference in my life.

Do you believe the Christian life is:

♦ Impossible to live.
♦ Impossible to live by yourself.
♦ Possible to live by yourself.
♦ Possible to live with Christ's strength.

Are you aware of having tried to practice self-control and failed?_____

_____

Examine the Scriptures and/or your answers in today's lesson. Determine the most meaningful thought for you today. Write your thought for the day here:

_____

_____

_____

_____

Applying what God is pointing out to you is essential. How will you apply this truth to your life today? _____

_____

_____

_____

Write a short prayer to God that summarizes your thoughts._____

_____

_____

_____

Did God bring to mind someone who needs to hear this truth? Who?_____

_____

Thought for the Day:

The Christian life is not difficult, but impossible to live on our own.

♦

D A Y   F O U R

The Work of the Spirit

Sin Has Not Been Eliminated as of the Date of Publication of this Book

For the wages of sin is death . . .
Romans 6:23, NKJV

. . . He will save His people from their sins.
Matthew 1:21, NKJV

One day I walked out to the plant with another engineer named Al. He said, "You seem to be happier lately, and you don't enter into the gripe sessions about the boss anymore. What happened?" He took me by surprise. I had no idea that there was any noticeable change since I had asked Christ to take away my anger. I made a feeble effort to explain my quest for help, but as a young Christian, I didn't understand what had happened very clearly myself.

"Can you help my wife and me? We are two miserable people," he said.

Well, my struggle had been very personal to me. I had no interest in getting involved in other people's lives. But his question was a challenge. Since I did research routinely as part of my work, I asked him to give me some time to study and research what had happened to me.

Respond to this often-made statement: "Well, I will just have to act tough and get through this difficulty. Things will get better with time." _____

_____

_____

Do you just try to act tough and make it through difficulties hoping time will heal your hurt? _____

How do you think you should respond when you find yourself making this statement?_____

_____

_____

_____

Finally, I had worked up a presentation and told him I was ready. My wife Eva and I invited Al and his wife to come to our house for one evening. When we sat down together, I reminded him that this "change" in my life only happened a few weeks ago. I had no idea how long it would last. Briefly, I told him that several years ago I had asked Jesus to come into my life and save me from my sins. Lately, I had asked Him to cleanse the anger and hate out of my heart, and as I understood it, He gave me the strength to be kind and tenderhearted on a daily basis.

I told them, "To tell the truth, I feel rather foolish telling you this. It seems as if I should be able to manage my own life, but I can't."

They both had tears in their eyes. They thought it was a wonderful story. I didn't want to get sidetracked from my presentation, so I said, "Let's look at what I have prepared."

I started out in the Garden of Eden. I took him through Moses' problems and the kings and the prophets (I wanted to be thorough). I touched on a few psalms. This took a couple of hours and pretty soon I moved into the New Testament and the gospel. I explained to them that Christ came into this world, and He loved the world so much that He died for us. And then I very generally asked them if they were ready to receive Christ. He said, "You know, I was ready an hour ago."

We all prayed rather awkwardly.

I have boiled my presentation down a little bit since then, but Al and Goldie became children of God and the first people I ever introduced to Jesus. Their marriage was healed. They became active in a church and never turned back. I still see Al occasionally. Goldie and Eva are with the Lord.

This experience with Al and Goldie opened up a whole new vista of opportunity for my wife and me that we never knew existed. We developed a hunger to know the Bible and share with other people. We had been going to church regularly and went to Sunday School, but in making preparation to talk with Al, I became aware of huge gaps in my biblical knowledge. The biggest gap was that I didn't know the meaning of sin.

If someone asked you to describe the meaning of sin, what would you tell them? _____

_____

_____

My wife and I began to do research into what the nature of sin is. We found the definition of sin in the dictionary: an offense against God. But we quickly discovered that the subject was broader and deeper than we ever dreamed it would be. In just five passages in the Bible we found over fifty sins listed. (See page 81 and appendix for a more complete list of sins and related Scriptures.)

Examine the Scriptures and/or your answers in today's lesson. Determine the most meaningful thought for you today. Write your thought for the day here:

_____

_____

_____

_____

Applying what God is pointing out to you is essential. How will you apply this truth to your life today? _____

_____

_____

Write a short prayer to God that summarizes your thoughts._____

_____

_____

_____

_____

Did God bring to mind someone who needs to hear this truth? Who?_____

_____

Thought for the Day:

If you don't know what sin is, you will inevitably suffer from its effects
and probably wonder why!

♦

DAY FIVE

The Nature of Sin

We grouped the sins against God into four categories in order to understand them (see table 2). The more we studied these lists, the more excited we became! We discovered that if we could eliminate our sins, we would solve most of our own problems and most of the ills of society, including the breakdown of the family, domestic violence, child abuse, rape, murder, violence, political deception, and personal misery. This table is based on Mark 7:21–23, Romans 1:28–31, Galatians 5:19–21, Ephesians 4:25–31, and 2 Timothy 3:1–5.

Evil thoughts, lust, and covetousness can lead to premarital sex and adultery. Lying, backbiting, quarreling, anger, and rebellion can lead to brutal violent behavior and even murder. Clearly someone with a brilliant mind who is consumed by greed, selfish ambition, and deception can devise ways to misuse the stock market or government funds.

I looked at these lists as a huge mirror and stepped up to it to see what it would reflect in me. Considering my past problems with my boss, my wife, and my child, it was hard to accept what I saw: evil thoughts, unthankfulness, pride, unforgiveness, deceitfulness, anger, bitterness, rebellion, lying, complaining, yelling, and quarreling. Imagine anyone walking around with all that inside. The simple yet profound statement that the blood of Jesus Christ can wash it all away is exciting! Is it really that simple? It is so easy that it insults our secular intelligence. Everyone, except those who try it, say: "That is much too simple." But the good news about these lists is that we are just a prayer away from help!

Table 2: Four Categories of Sins	
1. Sins of the Mind	evil thoughts unforgiveness unthankfulness selfish ambition pride deceitfulness covetousness greed lust
2. Sinful Emotions	jealousy anger malice envy bad temper unloving attitude hatred rebelliousness bitterness
3. Sins of the Mouth	lying backbiting complaining contentiousness disputing blaspheming slandering yelling boasting quarreling
4. Sins of Behavior	disobedience to parents brutality lack of self-control stealing adultery murder fornication violence drunkenness revelry

Take a few minutes now to stop and ask God if there is any sin in your life that you need to confess. Do not try to think up a sin; just ask God to show you if there is anything in your life that does not please Him. The Holy Spirit will reveal to you any sin. Write your list of sins on a piece of paper. Ask God to forgive you of them. Do you believe He did? _____

What will you begin doing now, or stop doing, that will show true repentance?

_____

_____

One Sunday morning I arrived early at the church where I was to speak. There was only one person in the auditorium. She was in front of the platform, arranging flowers in a basket. Perhaps a dozen varieties of flowers were masterfully arranged so that each flower was displayed at its best: colorful and delicate. The arrangement couldn't have been more beautiful.

My mind raced back to my boyhood. I could see my mother in her flower gardens. She just loved to raise many, many varieties of flowers. In those days, all I could see was flower beds that needed weeding. My mother could see magnificent baskets of masterfully arranged flowers gracing the platform of our church. Every Sunday during flower season, I had to share the back seat of the car with these bouquets. Mom was so excited at the chance to display God's magnificent creation for the praise and adoration of the Creator.

With my mother in mind, I approached the platform and said to the lady, "You surely have done a beautiful job arranging these flowers."

She turned around. I saw an angry-looking woman who growled, "I do it every Sunday. I am stuck with this job. No one else will do it. I'm sick and tired of getting up early enough to be the first one here." She wasn't really talking to me. She was venting an angry, rebellious spirit. She sputtered on to remark that no one appreciated her work.

"Who are you?" she asked, suddenly realizing that she was talking to a stranger. "I'm the visiting speaker," I replied. "Oh," she gasped, "Oh. Welcome to our church." It was an awkward, embarrassing moment for both of us. The mood of the moment didn't fit with the beauty of the flowers and the fragrance in the air.

Later, from the platform, I noticed the same lady. She seemed radiant and cheerful; a note in the bulletin gave her credit for the flowers. Even though she was deceptively charming, she was still suffering from the consequences of sin and didn't know it.

If she were to stand before the list of sins, she would need to check off anger, rebellion, deception. If she would repent and ask God to clean up her heart, she would be able to rejoice and enjoy the privilege of meeting with the Lord alone on Sunday mornings as she worships in His presence by working with the beautiful, fragrant flowers that He created.

What a pity to let sin steal away such a privilege when cleansing of the heart is just a prayer away.

The Bible cautioned us not to kid ourselves: "He who covers his sins will not prosper, but whoever confesses and forsakes them will have mercy" (Prov. 28:13, NKJV).

If you aren't going to call the list in this chapter sin, then you will look to the world around you for the cause and the solution for items on the list. But if it is sin, then you are looking at the simplest problem in the world to solve. You have the resources of the Creator of the world to help you. There is a supernatural cure for everyone. We don't have to avoid the problem or run away to try to get relief: "If we confess our sins, He is faithful and just to forgive us our sins and to cleanse us from all unrighteousness" (1 John 1:9, NKJV).

Are you a prayer away from help? _____

Examine the Scriptures and/or your answers in today's lesson. Determine the most meaningful thought for you today. Write your thought for the day here:

_____

_____

_____

_____

Applying what God is pointing out to you is essential. How will you apply this truth to your life today? _____

_____

_____

Write a short prayer to God that summarizes your thoughts._____

_____

_____

_____

_____

Did God bring to mind someone who needs to hear this truth? Who?_____

_____

Thought for the Day:
We are just a prayer away from victory over our sin.

♦

(Optional—But Recommended!)

Bring forward your thoughts from each day:

1. _____
2. _____
3. _____
4. _____
5. _____

Bring forward your application:

1. _____
2. _____
3. _____
4. _____
5. _____

Bring forward your prayers:

1. _____
2. _____
3. _____
4. _____
5. _____

Bring forward who you shared your thoughts with:

1. _____
2. _____
3. _____
4. _____
5. _____

Thought for the Week:

We tend to deny or ignore the existence of sin.

◆

1. See appendix for a more complete list of sins and related Scriptures.

UNIT FIVE

Why Don't You Just Concentrate on the Positive?

Thought Starter:

Is it difficult to deal with the negative in your life?

◆

Memory Verse for the Week:

Walk in the Spirit, and you shall not fulfill the lust of the flesh.
GALATIANS 5:16, NKJV

DAY ONE

The Positive of the Negative

My good friend, Dick Andrews, is a dentist. One day when I went to his office as a patient, I was startled to see him approach me with his hands in rubber gloves and a surgical mask covering his face.

"Are you going to operate?" I asked.

Through the mask he mumbled, "With the advent of AIDS, all dentists have adopted gloves and masks as routine protection." Dick proceeded to see if he could find some trouble in my mouth. By the time he had done some mysterious poking around, and his dental hygienist got through polishing my teeth, I walked out of there with gleaming, clean, healthy teeth. They looked for problems, and it was positive that he dealt with the negative.

Can you think of a negative that could be positive if you would just deal with it? _____

The physician also deals with negatives, yet he is one of the most respected people in the community. The way he helps us is to look for trouble and fix it. I experienced this in high school when I injured my knee while playing basketball. It was badly swollen and just barely fit into my pants leg. I had to keep it bent to ease the pain. I hobbled into the team physician's office on crutches. He said, "You have a bad knee." He didn't even mention my good knee or the rest of my healthy body. (Is that negative?)

He said, "Stretch your leg out on this table," and ignored the fact that this caused me excruciating pain. He began to thump my knee, asking me where it hurt the most. When he found that spot, he thumped it some more to be sure. Then he smiled, "We will need to lance it. This will hurt." Sweat poured out all over my body from the pain. Then he plunged a knife into my swollen knee. Lots of nasty stuff poured out. I had never felt such pain before! But my knee did get better.

It was positive that he dealt with the negative.

The physician and the dentist are members of professions we hold in high esteem. Yet, their focus is on finding trouble in your body:

"You have two cavities."

"You have an abscess in your knee."

The comforting side of their professions is that when they find out what is wrong, they proceed to fix it. They can only help us as they deal with the negative.

Actually, much of society focuses on correcting or preventing the negative: firemen, police, auto mechanics, physicians, lawyers, dentists, laboratories, and many others. You can imagine the results if a fireman ignored a fire or a doctor only wanted to focus on my good leg. Even in the field of counseling we usually study the problems of clients; we don't spend a lot of time studying happy, contented people. In sports, if you want to be good, you locate a coach who will study what you are doing wrong so you can eliminate that flaw in your performance. So it is with our spiritual lives. We need to deal with the negative.

The psalmist prayed: "Search me, O God, and know my heart; try me, and know my thoughts: and see if there be any wicked way in me, and lead me in the way everlasting" (Ps. 139:23–24, KJV).

In order to be healthy, spiritually speaking, we also need to look for trouble, a sinful condition in the body, so it can be fixed. The Bible says: "Walk in the Spirit, and you shall not fulfill the lust of the flesh" (Gal. 5:16, NKJV).

While my wife and I were researching the subject of sin we also discovered lists that describe the fruit of the Spirit. Look at Table 3 for differences in living while being filled with the Spirit and in living a "normal" life with sin in control.

These are based on Mark 7:21–23, Romans 1:28–31, Galatians 5:19–21, Ephesians 4:25–31, and 2 Timothy 3:1–5.

Most people would agree that walking in the Spirit is a superior way to live, but, realistically, a miracle is needed to actually live this way. Fortunately, the power to walk in the Spirit comes from God. And no human beings or circumstances can interrupt your relationship with Him.

We all have a choice. The Bible says: "In the past you voluntarily gave your bodies to the service of vice and wickedness—for the purpose of becoming wicked. So, now, give yourselves to the service of righteousness—for the purpose of becoming really good,"(Rom. 6:19, PHILLIPS).

If you want to enlarge your knowledge of God's resources, look at these verses:

To those who through the righteousness of our God and Savior Jesus Christ have received a faith as precious as ours: Grace and peace be yours in abundance through the knowledge of God and of Jesus our Lord. His divine power has given us everything we need for life and godliness through our knowledge of him who called us by his own glory and goodness. Through these he has given us his very great and precious promises, so that through them you may participate in the divine nature and escape the corruption in the world caused by evil desires (2 Pet. 1:2–4).

May the God of hope fill you will all joy and peace as you trust in him, so that you may overflow with hope by the power of the Holy Spirit (Rom. 15:13).

Grace and peace to you from God our Father and the Lord Jesus Christ. Praise be to the God and Father of our Lord Jesus Christ, the Father of compassion and the God of all comfort, who comforts us in all our troubles, so that we can comfort those in any trouble with the comfort we ourselves have received from God (2 Cor. 1:2–4).

Being strengthened with all power according to his glorious might so that you may have great endurance and patience (Col. 1:11).

May the Lord make your love increase and overflow for each other and for everyone else, just as ours does for you (1 Thess. 3:12).

But the wisdom that comes from heaven is first of all pure; then peace loving, considerate, submissive, full of mercy and good fruit, impartial and sincere. Peacemakers who sow in peace raise a harvest of righteousness (James 3:17–18).

Only God can cleanse us from sin and empower us to walk in the spirit. Good news: we are free to choose.

Pretend that the chart on page 81 is a mirror. What do you see? _____

_____

_____

_____

_____

_____

Table 3: Spirit-Controlled Living vs. Sin-Controlled Living			
Spirit-Filled Mind		Sins of the Mind	
forgiveness hope appreciation willingness impartiality	humility thankfulness confidence wisdom	unforgiveness evil thoughts covetousness greed lust	pride ingratitude selfish ambition deceitfulness
Spirit-Filled Emotions		Sinful Emotions	
love peace gentle spirit gladness	joy long-suffering kindly spirit	hatred rebellion bitterness envy bad temper	anger unloving attitude jealousy malice
Spirit-Filled Mouth		Sins of the Mouth	
truthfulness thankfulness gentle answer encouraging tact	praise timeliness soothing tongue pleasant words	lying complaining yelling contentiousness boasting	slandering disputing backbiting quarrelsomeness blasphemy
Spirit-Filled Behavior		Sins of Behavior	
kindness righteousness obedience goodness courage	gentleness self-control cooperation sincerity servant	fornication adultery drunkenness murder revelry	brutality without self-control stealing violence disobedience to parents

Examine the Scriptures and/or your answers in today's lesson. Determine the most meaningful thought for you today. Write your thought for the day here:

_____

_____

_____

_____

Applying what God is pointing out to you is essential. How will you apply this truth to your life today? _____

_____

_____

Write a short prayer to God that summarizes your thoughts._____

_____

_____

_____

_____

Did God bring to mind someone who needs to hear this truth? Who?_____

_____

Thought for the Day:

It is negative to ignore the negative; it is positive to eliminate the negative.

◆

DAY TWO

So be careful. If you are thinking, "Oh, I would never behave like that"—let this be a warning to you. For you too may fall into sin.
1 CORINTHIANS 10:12, TLB

Look! Do You Want to Drive This Car, or Do You Want Me to Do It?

Throughout life I have tended to resist facing up to my sinful behavior when I was in the middle of doing it. Often, to have my sinful behavior pointed out to me was more distressing than the behavior itself. This graphically happened to me once in a manner that I will never forget.

I was speaking fervently one night on confession and repentance. After the meeting, my wife and I drove awhile to our next engagement. We stopped to spend the night in a first-class hotel. We slept on the finest mattress money could buy. In the morning we had baths and used the deodorants that the ads say you should use to promote good will. We had a good breakfast. We started out in our new, air-conditioned car, complete with stereo radio.

Humanly speaking, we had to have a good day, didn't we? According to the sociologists, we had a good secure environment, we were well-educated, challenged, enjoyed good housing, good food, we were clean, and we had money. We had it made, didn't we?

It was a beautiful day and all was friendly until we came to a crossroad leading on to the freeway. I turned toward Detroit, our destination, when my wife said, "Henry, you are going the wrong way."

That remark burned me up. My caustic reply was, "Don't you think I know where Detroit is? Look! Do you want to drive this car, or do you want me to do it?!"

And away we went in air-conditioned comfort. We still smelled good. We had a good breakfast under our belts, we had nice clothes, the scenery was beautiful, the car was driving smoothly, and *I was furious.* Telling me that I was headed in the wrong direction! I'd lived in this area for years and surely knew my directions! After all, when you feel deeply and certain about something, you ought to stick up for your convictions, shouldn't you? She said nothing. She was to handle the road map and keep us from getting lost.

After a while we came to the first exit. A huge sign with an arrow pointed in the direction we were going. Above the arrow was the word *Chicago.* That was the opposite direction from Detroit.

Now, I have a Ph.D. degree. My training is in the area of evaluating data unemotionally and accurately to produce advice based on the data. This is how I make my living. I get paid for my judgments.

I chose to ignore the sign.

Away we went, in air-conditioned comfort. We came to the next exit, which was some distance from the last one. The sign had a big arrow pointing in our direction, and above the arrow: *Chicago.*

Did you ever get that cold, clammy feeling after you have set someone straight that it's possible that you might be wrong? I felt myself becoming more angry *at my wife* and decided to try one more exit, and away we went.

What advice would you give if someone acted like this? _____

_____

_____

_____

Can you believe that? You smile, but do you realize that you are smiling at a very sad story? What does this illustrate? The weaknesses and limitations of education. Is it not true that in a fit of anger and stubbornness, all you know can get short-circuited and you can act like a stupid fool?

A brittle, electric silence was in the air. Both of us looked straight ahead and were silent.

The next exit was the same. There was that arrow pointing to Chicago. Would you believe that I decided to try one more exit in order to give me time to figure out how to get to Detroit without turning around.

Have you ever acted like that? You know you are wrong, but, so help you, you are not going to admit it. You do everything you can to avoid admitting you are wrong. That is the way it was with me. You couldn't have dragged me off that freeway with a tow truck!

I shared this story of my driving past exits with a close friend for his comments before submitting the manuscript for publication. He told me that I needed to reduce the number of exits that I drove past. He said that one or two would be okay, but passing three exits would stretch my creditability and was out of the question. He pointed out that, in his opinion, it also insulted the intelligence of the reader.

I gave his suggestion serious thought and decided that his constructive comments were logical and correct. But, over the next few days, I kept thinking, "But it is a true story!" Then it hit me: My behavior only reinforces the lesson! We as Christians tend to underestimate sin's power over our behavior. I kept the original story.

Human emotions can totally disengage our brain, preventing rational behavior and acceptance of the fact that we sin. I have seen this in my own life and in those of my clients.

Can you remember the last time you were wrong but yet would not admit it? Write down your answer. _____

_____

Sin's power doesn't make us a ridiculous offer! Sin's power gives us the opportunity to be like we want whether it is right or not!

An intelligent man nearly destroyed his marriage and family by repeatedly overworking. He was a wealthy, successful lawyer who didn't need to work at all if he didn't wish.

Another client came panting into my office and wearily lowered himself into a chair. He was at least one hundred pounds overweight. He called himself a compulsive eater. He was a physician.

A beautiful, frightened lady was clasping and unclasping her hands as she told me how worried she was about AIDS. She was sexually active.

An affluent couple anxiously asked me for help with a teenage daughter who was on drugs and sexually active. Against their better judgment, they had showered her with money, cars, and clothes for years.

A skeleton of a young lady looked hopelessly forlorn sitting straight in her chair; she was bulimic and starving herself. She was on the honor roll in school.

I find that I must constantly remind myself, again and again, never to underestimate the power of sin to short-circuit my intelligence.

How do you get turned around when you are headed in the wrong direction? The Bible says: "If we confess our sins, He is faithful and just to forgive us our sins and to cleanse us from all unrighteousness" (1 John 1:9, NKJV).

I have learned from the Bible that:

Repentance is a five-step process:

1. **I am wrong.**
2. **I am sorry.**
3. **Forgive me.**
4. **Cleanse me.**
5. **Empower me.**

These steps are so important that they will be examined one at a time in the next daily assignments.

Examine the Scriptures and/or your answers in today's lesson. Determine the most meaningful thought for you today. Write your thought for the day here:

_____

_____

_____

Applying what God is pointing out to you is essential. How will you apply this truth to your life today? _____

_____

Write a short prayer to God that summarizes your thoughts._____

_____

_____

_____

Did God bring to mind someone who needs to hear this truth? Who?_____

_____

Thought for the Day:

We tend to ignore or deny our sin.

◆

DAY THREE

For everyone practicing evil hates the light and does not come to the light, lest his deeds should be exposed.
JOHN 3:20, NKJV

Why Is It Difficult to Say, "I Am Wrong; I Have Sinned"?

How do you get turned around when you are headed in the wrong direction? I'm three-and-a-half exits down the road. There are no questions at this point: We are headed in the wrong direction; I blew up at my wife for trying to help; and I even tried to tell her that she was wrong. What to do?

How often do you hear someone say: "I am wrong. I have sinned"? Instead, I hear people declare that they are unhappy, tense, anxious, worried, disappointed, misunderstood, mistrusted, unloved, or under extreme pressure.

Frequently I listen to highly intelligent, competent, educated, successful people say the strangest things, such as:

♦ "I blew up," or "I exploded." People say this very sincerely. Of course this never happens. Picture a person who blew up: teeth, bones, eyeballs, arms, legs, body parts flying in all directions.

♦ "I broke down." Can you see this quivering, helpless body collapsed in a heap?

♦ "I lost my head." Can you picture such an unlikely sight of a headless person groping around?

♦ "She gets under my skin." One can accept the presence of a microscopic creature having entered the body, but hardly a full-grown woman.

◆ "My blood was boiling." This person is no doubt experiencing some bodily changes, but hardly the condition described here.

◆ "I was beside myself." This statement simply defies logic.

◆ "He turns me on."

◆ "He turns me off."

◆ "He burns me up."

◆ "He turns me cold."

◆ "I am fed up."

Can you think of other excuses? _____

_____

_____

My purpose in recording these statements is not to belittle anyone or to treat their reports lightly. These are socially acceptable terms describing bodily changes that we are aware of as we interact with people and respond to the events of the day.

We freely describe ourselves and our problems as being caused by other people. But it is very difficult to say the simple words, "I am wrong. I have sinned."

If I say, "I am wrong; I have sinned," I can then cure the problems. The problems cannot be solved any other way.

The big little word is *if*. That word represents a major hurdle because I have a tendency to say things like: "I *may* have been off base, but I have some good points about me. Haven't I been faithful in teaching biblical principles worldwide? Haven't I worked hard at being a good husband and father? Don't I get some points for providing a good home?"

None of my past history helped at this point.

I am three-and-a-half exits down the pike and going in the wrong direction. That fact couldn't be sidestepped.

When I share this story of driving down the freeway with audiences, I say, "Now sin is doing wrong according to God's standard. What were my sins? Can you help me out?"

Read the following and check the box that describes you.

❑ I don't believe that people can see other people's sin very easily.

❑ I always see where I am wrong and stop my actions immediately.

❑ I want to become more sensitive to when I sin so that I may correct the negative with God and get on with the positive.

Without exception, the ladies in the audience always respond immediately and with the same words: pride, stubbornness, rebellion, impoliteness, anger, and bullheadedness.

I reply, "What are you doing diagnosing me? You are not trained, are you? The point is that it is not that hard to figure out what my sins were. You can tick them off, boom, boom, boom, and you are quickly and accurately diagnosing my problem."

Clearly I am wrong on two points: the list of words that accurately describes the condition "under my skin" and the fact that I am going the wrong direction on the freeway.

Now it is important to understand that I could acknowledge being wrong on all points without agreeing that I have sinned against God. It is important to comprehend that being wrong and being sinful are not interchangeable words. We must be clear on what we mean by being wrong.

I always ask my audiences after they volunteer the words above: "Are you telling me what you think I want to hear, or do you really believe these words are sins?"

How can an audience diagnose my sins so quickly? Look, all of us are familiar with such behavior.

I have noticed the same process in the consulting room. A counselee seldom has any problem describing someone else's weakness or unacceptable behavior. Their memory also serves them well in recalling past instances when someone mistreated them.

To face personal wrongdoing is a different matter. I seldom hear anyone eagerly volunteering information about their own wrongdoings.

But, if it is sin, then there is no human remedy. The cure to the problem involves a miracle and what must happen goes against our human nature

Step 1: I must confess "I am wrong; I have sinned."

The Bible tells us how to get turned around: "If we confess our sins, He is faithful and just to forgive our sins and to cleanse us from all unrighteousness" (1 John 1:9, NKJV).

I need to realize that I am wrong because I have sinned against God's standard. My words and emotional response to my wife's statement were wrong and sin.

As I was driving down the freeway, I realized I was proud (too proud to admit I was wrong), stubborn, rebellious, impolite, and angry. That's hard to admit. To call this response *sin* is even harder. I tend to turn away from this description of myself. It is embarrassing. We always seem to ask, "Isn't there a more palatable explanation?"

The Bible records a midnight conversation between Jesus and Nicodemus, the dean of the theological school. Jesus was explaining why people struggle with guilt. He said:

> **This is the condemnation, that the light has come into the world, and men loved darkness rather than light, because their deeds were evil. For everyone practicing evil hates the light and does not come to the light, lest his deeds should be exposed. But he who does the truth comes to the light, that his deeds may be clearly seen, that they have been done in God.**
>
> JOHN 3:19-21, NKJV

Hear me! It took me four exits to admit that I'm a bullheaded, stubborn, proud, angry person. I don't like that. And my wife had better not tell me that. But, as a counselor who has spent over forty years of my life working to help people, I have observed that it is very, very difficult to take the first step toward the cure, which is admitting, "I am wrong."

Isn't it often true that before we get turned around to face the truth, we are way down the road somewhere? We must all submit to the same treatment if we are to be cured.

But I have found that when there is a crisis, it's easy to get preoccupied with the other person's sins. When you think of somebody that you're at odds with, can you not think of all the things that are wrong with them? You can even pray for them, "Oh, God, straighten them out." Face it! We all tend to deny our sins.

I must talk to God about my own sins and admit that simple but difficult point, "I am wrong," regardless of the other person's problems.

Take a few minutes to stop now and pray. Ask God to help you see yourself as He sees you. Ask God to show you your sin so that you can receive cleansing, and curing grace. After you pray, write what you experienced. _____

_____

_____

What is the first step in curing the problem?
I must _____; "I am _____; I have _____."

Examine the Scriptures and/or your answers in today's lesson. Determine the most meaningful thought for you today. Write your thought for the day here:

_____

_____

_____

Applying what God is pointing out to you is essential. How will you apply this truth to your life today? _____

_____

Write a short prayer to God that summarizes your thoughts. _____

_____

_____

_____

Did God bring to mind someone who needs to hear this truth? Who?_____

_____

Thoughts for the Day:

Recognizing your sin is the first step toward a cure.

————

Ignoring your sin and recognizing another's sin only delays the cure to your problem.

◆

D A Y   F O U R

I Must Confess

Yes, but . . . why is it so important to always get to tell our side of the story?

If to acknowledge sinful behavior is a struggle, to be sorry about it is more of a struggle. Routinely, people ask for a chance to explain their behavior. Then they proceed to describe external circumstances that explain their behavior and make statements such as:

- ◆ "Lord, I'm mad and angry and bullheaded, but who wouldn't be with a spouse like that!?"
- ◆ "The boss yelled at me, and he didn't have his facts straight."
- ◆ "The kids kept fighting."
- ◆ "You drove me to it."
- ◆ "I haven't been getting enough sleep."
- ◆ "I grew up in a bad neighborhood."
- ◆ "I haven't been feeling well lately."
- ◆ "Let me tell you about the problems my family had . . ."
- ◆ "My parents didn't love or understand me."
- ◆ "Lord, this is the way I am, but you know how hard I've tried to serve you."

Do these statements sound familiar? You see, I can announce that that's the way I am, but then I want to blame someone else or some circumstances in my life or my background.

Jesus once declared to a group of religious leaders, "You . . . justify yourselves before men, but God knows your hearts" (Luke 16:15, NKJV).

Human behavior has not changed over recorded history, and the next step in repenting is just as difficult today as it was in Jesus' time.

Step 2: I need to say to God: "I am sorry. I have sinned."

Obviously, you can confess to having done something sinful and not be the least bit sorry to God. You may even be purposing in your heart to repeat the same behavior. Or you may be sorry you were caught, because now you will suffer the consequences of your actions. Other times we can sin and apologize to an individual, but leave God completely out of the situation.

The apostle Paul wrote to the Corinthians rebuking them for mixing with idolaters. He describes their response to his first letter:

> Now I rejoice, not that you were made sorry, but that your sorrow led to repentance. For you were made sorry in a godly manner, that you might suffer loss from us in nothing. For godly sorrow produces repentance to salvation, not to be regretted; but the sorrow of the world produces death. For observe this very thing, that you sorrowed in a godly manner: What diligence it produced in you, what clearing of yourselves, what indignation, what fear, what vehement desire, what zeal, what vindication!
>
> 2 Corinthians 7:9–11, NKJV

It's a struggle to come to the place where I can say, "I am wrong. I have sinned. No excuses, no alibis. This is *my* sin and I mean it. I am sorry, God."

Admitting sinful behavior and expressing sorrow for that behavior is something that we do reluctantly. We find that it's a struggle to let go of the reasons why our behavior is someone else's fault.

Perhaps more sins need to be dealt with that haven't been acknowledged. Perhaps we do not really accept the fact that our behavior was sinful.

What is the second step in curing the problem?
I need to say to God: "I am _____; I have _____."

Step 3: I need to ask: "God, forgive me of my sins."

I'm Not Good Enough Right Now!
Why am I uncomfortable when I think about asking to be forgiven?

When we finally relinquish our excuses, a strange thing often happens: rather than seeking forgiveness, we want to do penance for our sins. Sometimes, we even focus on how sinful we have been; memories crowd in of unpleasant scenes. Instead of seeking forgiveness, which is something God does for us, we find ourselves dwelling on the past. As a result, I hear statements such as:

- "Can't you see I am crying?"
- "Can't you see I'm depressed?"
- "My self-esteem is destroyed!"
- "I hate myself."
- "I am unworthy."
- "My self-image is battered."

More likely we need to review the good news that Jesus shed His blood for our sins to make the free gift of forgiveness available to us. We just need to receive it.

Let me remind you that this encounter is directly between us and God. Only He can forgive and cleanse sin. Step 1 of confession and step 2 of sorrow are things that I do. Asking for forgiveness is something I also do, but the forgiving is something that only God does. As the apostle John affirms: "If we confess our sins, He is faithful and just to forgive us our sins and to cleanse us from all unrighteousness" (1 John 1:9, NKJV).

So, none of the penance programs will help. God simply expects us to receive His forgiveness. It's free. His Son shed His blood to make this free gift available to us. I need to accept the cure for my past sin and say, "God, forgive me of my sin."

I find it interesting that Jesus *spoke* and the sick were healed. He *spoke* and the man's sins were forgiven. When we sincerely *say,* "God, forgive me of my sins," He does!

What is the third step in curing the problem?
I need to ask: "God, _____ me of my _____."

Examine the Scriptures and/or your answers in today's lesson. Determine the most meaningful thought for you today. Write your thought for the day here:

_____

_____

_____

_____

Applying what God is pointing out to you is essential. How will you apply this truth to your life today? _____

_____

Write a short prayer to God that summarizes your thoughts._____

_____

_____

_____

_____

Did God bring to mind someone who needs to hear this truth? Who?_____

_____

Thoughts for the Day:

I tend to justify my sin instead of being sorry to God for it.

————

It is a struggle to accept my own sin and say, "I sinned; I am wrong."

♦

DAY FIVE

Repentance Is a Cure

Now That I Know, I'll Do It!

If I do what I'm supposed to do as a Christian, isn't that enough? We identify our sins and seek forgiveness. John goes further and directs us: "But if we walk in the light as He is in the light, we have fellowship with one another, and the blood of Jesus Christ His Son cleanseth us from all sin" (1 John 1:7, NKJV).

Step 4: I need to ask: "God, cleanse me of my sins."

My sins were pride, stubbornness, rebellion, anger, and impoliteness. "Cleanse me" sounds easy. However, I have observed this to be extremely difficult for many people, especially talented, educated, self-sufficient, independent people. Our tendency is to put confidence in self-control rather than surrender to God. We say, "Now that I know what the problem is, I'll take charge and fix it" or "Just tell me what I'm supposed to do and I'll do it."

Sometimes we are still not convinced that we have sinned. We take another try at disciplining ourselves to act the way we think a Christian should act. The sin area is still there, and there is no cure at this time, only the counterfeit appearance of a cure. We keep saying: "There must be *something* I can do!"

Not this time. If it is sin, there is no human remedy. Give it up. You have admitted your sin, expressed sorrow, and asked for forgiveness. Now, receive the cleansing. Be specific about what needs cleansing in your life and know that only God can cleanse you from sin.

What is the fourth step in curing the problem?
I need to ask: "God, _____ me of my sins."

Is God a crutch that I need for the rest of my life?

Step 5: I need to ask: "Empower me."
Step 5 is the toughest step of all. It's not a matter of receiving a boost from God to get us started so we can proceed on our own. This step involves the realization that we will be dependent on God forever, not only to cleanse us from sin, but to empower us to keep His commandments in the future.

Intelligent, competent, successful people find this a hard pill to swallow. Our human nature causes us to resist the necessity for a lifetime dependence on God to correct our tendency to sin. And if it's sin, there is no human cure.

For Christians to try to live the Christian life without total dependence on the Holy Spirit is a contradiction in terms. Anything less is just acting. Paul's words are true: "And my God shall supply all your need according to His riches in glory by Christ Jesus" (Phil. 4:19, NKJV) and ". . . be filled with the Spirit" (Eph. 5:18, NKJV).

We want to be self-sufficient and independent. Many people have enough self-control to act the way they choose to act. They can rightly say, "Now that I know what to do, I will act like a Christian." They think they are in total control of their own lives. What they have is only a sad counterfeit that appears to be a cure.

To be clean, forgiven, and renewed is a great relief. Now it is time to turn around.

In my story of driving down the freeway, we were three-and-a-half exits down the pike. Isn't it amazing how long we will fight the truth? Finally I was ready to reach out to God for help. I had to admit to my proud, rebellious, angry, stubborn spirit. My wife can't help me here. She can't cure me. I must deal with God. I asked God to cleanse my heart, to restore His love, peace and joy to my heart, to help me face the truth. Guess what? He answered my prayer. Up to that point you could not have dragged me off that freeway. Now, the most delightful thought in my mind was to look for the next exit. I am free from the effects of my sins. Happy thought. I could turn around.

"Eva," I said, "we are headed in the wrong direction" *(as if she didn't know)*. "I am sorry. Forgive me." It was now easy to admit the truth.

Soon we came to the next exit. We turned around and drove all the way back. And that's sometimes the trail of repentance; we retrace a lot of steps and make some corrections along the way. There is no other way to start fresh and clean.

Examine this scripture verse:

> **I preached that they should repent and turn to God and prove their repentance by their deeds.**
>
> ACTS 26:20, NIV

What do you see from the Scripture that shows repentance has taken place?

_____

How difficult is it for you not only to admit that you are wrong, but turn around and begin doing works of righteousness? _____

Personally, I find that I need to frequently repeat these steps. And the mystery is that one can be determined to be consciously wrong, no matter what, and then, in response to a repentant prayer, be transformed into a person who delights in being consciously right.

What is the fifth step in curing the problem?
I need to ask: "_____ me."

The Process of Repentance

I have broken down the term repentance into five steps. Actually, as we practice this process daily, these steps merge into a smooth process that is like one step. It's like driving a car. A beginner is conscious of the brake, accelerator, speedometer, side mirror, windows, and rear-view mirror. Gradually all these activities merge into one motion.

To confess and repent can be as simple as slowing down for a driver who is committed to driving the speed limit.

As a young Christian (and even to this day), I was astounded at the reluctance of people (including me) to face up to their sins. To bring up the subject creates an atmosphere of resistance, tension, anxiety, and anger.

You would think that everyone would leap at the chance to be rid of sin. Not so. Usually, people do not seek a real cure to their problems (sins); they just want relief from the consequences of their sins.

Are you one of those people who resists facing up to your sin?

❏ Yes
❏ No
❏ I'm not sure. However, I really do want to learn how to face up to my sin.

I'm not some stranger to this material. I'm the one that is teaching and practicing it. But between conferences, look what happened. I don't always know why it happens, but when it does I need to call it by its right name: sin. In my case, I not only blew up at my wife, but I also tried to tell her she was wrong! To admit our own sin is very difficult for all of us because sin has a way of short-circuiting our brain.

This word *sin* is seldom heard; it is despised, dreaded and hated. Newspapers scream daily about problems that fit the definition, but they refuse to call it by the right name. Society doesn't put sin into you; it stirs up what is already there. If it is sin, there is no human remedy.

A supernatural cure for sin is available. I can only experience consistent peace, joy, and love when the Holy Spirit is in control of my life.

It is thought-provoking that we have available a supernatural cure for sin, but the whole subject is resisted and its cure is rejected.

Scan the column headings of your newspaper for a dozen examples of social behavior. List your findings here:_____

_____

_____

_____

Examine the Scriptures and/or your answers in today's lesson. Determine the most meaningful thought for you today. Write your thought for the day here:

_____

_____

_____

Applying what God is pointing out to you is essential. How will you apply this truth to your life today? _____

_____

Write a short prayer to God that summarizes your thoughts._____

_____

_____

_____

Did God bring to mind someone who needs to hear this truth? Who?_____

_____

Review the 5-Step Process To Repentance:

1. I confess "I am wrong. I have sinned."
2. I say to God, "I am sorry. I have sinned."
3. I ask, "God, forgive me of my sins."
4. I ask, "God, cleanse me of my sins."
5. I ask, "God, empower me."

After you have dealt with God concerning your sin, then you must correct the relationship with any person you may have offended. Personalizing steps one, two, and three will help you in knowing how to correct the injured relationship.

Thought for the Day:

Repentance brings a cure for sin, not just relief from symptoms.

◆

(Optional—But Recommended!)

Bring forward your thoughts from each day:

1. _____
2. _____
3. _____
4. _____
5. _____

Bring forward your application:

1. _____
2. _____
3. _____
4. _____
5. _____

Bring forward your prayers:

1. _____
2. _____
3. _____
4. _____
5. _____

Bring forward who you shared your thoughts with:

1. _____

2. _____

3. _____

4. _____

5. _____

Thought for the Week:

To correct our tendency to sin requires a life-time dependence on God.

◆

UNIT SIX

Why Is It Difficult to Walk by a Mirror Without Looking at Yourself?

Thought Starter:

Is the real you underneath your skin?

◆

Memory Verse for the Week:

Man looks at the outward appearance, but the Lord looks at the heart.
1 SAMUEL 16:7, NKJV

DAY ONE

Take heed to thyself, and keep thy soul diligently.
DEUTERONOMY 4:9, KJV

Soul Check

When people come into my consulting room, I can see that they have taken time to look nice. However, what we talk about is the part of them you can't see, the world of thoughts, feelings, and emotions underneath the skin. This part of us that no one can see is what some call the soul.

Very few of us would think of neglecting our appearance before leaving home. We want to make the image we see reflected in the mirror acceptable to ourselves and others. We know that others make judgments about us based on our appearance.

Very few people get to see what we see in the mirror in the morning. What people do see is our version of what we want them to see. Some people have more work to do than others.

Multi-million dollar industries provide products for eye care, ear care, lip care, hair care, body care, and clothing.

As you look in the mirror in the morning, you are vaguely aware of your behavior patterns, thoughts, and reactions. Circumstances and events in your life make you aware of pleasant or unpleasant thoughts and emotions. And as you look in the mirror, you are either pleased or displeased with yourself.

With personal behavior, as with personal appearance, you behave acceptably to particular persons or groups. In their presence, regardless of what they say or do, regardless of the reactions going on underneath the skin, you strive diligently to maintain a pleasant smile, a friendly word, and a congenial manner.

Few people get to see what you see in the mirror, and no one gets to see what goes on underneath your skin except God. The Bible says: "Man looks at the outward appearance, but the Lord looks at the heart" (1 Sam. 16:7, NKJV).

If the Lord looks on the heart, then it follows that a checkup of your heart is more critical than an examination of your physical appearance.

I don't like checkups. I usually have a feeling of uneasiness and uncertainty that something bad will come up that I don't know about. When a physician checks your body, he is alert to discover anything that needs correcting.

Soul-searching can be as uncomfortable as a physical checkup. But if God looks upon the heart, one needs to be sure of His approval. The psalmist said: "Search me, O God, and know my heart; try me, and know my thoughts: And see if there be any wicked way in me." (Psalm 139:23–24, KJV).

How often do you have a soul check?
- ❏ Every Day
- ❏ Usually
- ❏ Sometimes
- ❏ Seldom
- ❏ Never

How does the time spent on your outward appearance compare to the time spent on inward preparation? _____

_____

What basis do you use for checking up on your soul? _____

_____

_____

When Moses passed the mantle of leadership to Joshua, he said to the people: "Give heed to yourself and keep your soul diligently, lest you forget the things which your eyes have seen, and lest they depart from your heart all the days of your life" (Deut. 4:9, NASB).

Most of us don't need any urging to look after our personal appearances and personal advantages. We encounter people every day, and their approval or disapproval is face to face and immediate.

Examine the Scriptures and/or your answers in today's lesson. Determine the most meaningful thought for you today. Write your thought for the day here:

_____

_____

_____

Applying what God is pointing out to you is essential. How will you apply this truth to your life today? _____

_____

_____

Write a short prayer to God that summarizes your thoughts._____

_____

_____

_____

_____

Did God bring to mind someone who needs to hear this truth? Who?_____

_____

Thought for the Day:

Learn to check the appearance of your soul every day just as
willingly as you check your physical appearance.

◆

D A Y   T W O

A Root of Bitterness Unchecked

It is fairly simple to lose sight of the need for the Lord's approval. The effects of deviating from His standards may not be evident to you and others for a long time. As a result, more and more frequently these days I hear about another "model" couple who, after twenty years of marriage, are getting a divorce.

One such marriage might have been saved if they had heeded this biblical advice: "Looking diligently lest anyone fall short of the grace of God; lest any root of bitterness springing up cause trouble, and by this many become defiled" (Heb. 12:15, NKJV).

I was sure that this couple had a marriage that was grounded solidly on mutual devotion to each other. He had poured twelve years of his life into a service organization. He worked long and sacrificially, and his wife was by his side, supporting him. We all admired their commitment and even thought of them as a model couple who put serving the Lord as the top priority in their lives.

Then we heard the chilling news that he had resigned from the organization, was divorcing his wife, and would marry another woman. Everyone was shocked; all of a sudden this model marriage just collapsed. I had a chance to talk to him about the surprise development. He was quick to assure me, however, that there was nothing sudden about it. This break had been coming on for years.

He and his wife encountered conflict from the beginning of their marriage. The first issue was over money; she failed to record checks she had written. The monthly bank statements were consistently different from his checkbook. He brought the matter up repeatedly; she ignored the problem. After a few years he quit trying, but a root of bitterness developed in his heart.

There were other issues. One was a running battle about punctuality. They differed over rules for their two teenagers. Another issue was the level of involvement with their immediate families. These issues had rocked along unresolved for seventeen years.

Strangely enough, they had worked together on one project, creating the impression around friends and associates that they were a happy, cooperative couple. But in reality, skillful deception covered growing bitterness.

Eventually his work on a certain committee placed him next to a rather plain woman. He helped her into her chair and at the break he served her coffee. Nothing unusual about that. At the next meeting he arrived early, as was his custom. He was the first one there, and the second one, also early, was the woman who had sat next to him. He complimented her on being early. She replied that this was her custom, but when she went to meetings with her husband, they were always late. He remarked that he and his wife had the same problem. She complimented him on his attentiveness, remarking that her husband never paid much attention to such things.

What advice would you give this man or woman at this point of the relationship? _____

_____

_____

_____

He was given responsibility for producing a report, and she was appointed to help him with research and typing. She was prompt and cooperative. He remarked that he wished his wife would work with him like that. He found himself thinking about this woman frequently. Once, they had lunch together to plan their report. His hand brushed hers and lingered there.

She began telling him about other problems she had involving her husband. He sympathized with her because he, too, had some problems with his wife. After lunch, she took his arm as they walked to her car. He found himself thinking about her in the office, and on an impulse, called her and offered to pick her up for the next committee meeting. After driving her home, they sat in front of her house and chatted awhile. He walked her to the door and gave her hand a squeeze as he said good-bye. After the next meeting, they spontaneously kissed, which was an electrifying experience that he hadn't enjoyed for a long time.

What these two people had in common was a root of bitterness. As a result, they had forgotten the sweet times in their marriages, and any grace toward their partners had departed from their hearts. Along with the bitterness, uncontrollable lust flared up. From that point, reason went out the window and before they recovered, they had broken up two marriages, ruined two careers, and ended up married to each other. They soon found out that they had new conflicts to deal with in each other.

Since then, they have come to their senses, have sought God's forgiveness, and are trying to repair the damage that has been done. They are finding out that they have no good options, but must make the best of a hopeless mess: two successful careers and two marriages died.

Important Lesson: The greater the gap between outward behavior and the condition underneath your skin (hypocrisy), the greater the possibility of deceiving yourself.

The Bible says: "Do not merely listen to the word, and so deceive yourselves. Do what it says" (James 1:22).

Examine the Scriptures and/or your answers in today's lesson. Determine the most meaningful thought for you today. Write your thought for the day here:

_____

_____

_____

_____

_____

Applying what God is pointing out to you is essential. How will you apply this truth to your life today? _____

_____

_____

_____

Write a short prayer to God that summarizes your thoughts._____

_____

_____

_____

_____

Did God bring to mind someone who needs to hear this truth? Who?_____

_____

Thought for the Day:

A root of bitterness can twist your thinking and make something wrong seem beautiful.

◆

D A Y   T H R E E

A Checkup for the Soul

What happened? This man and this woman had neglected to check up on their souls.

A checkup of the soul need not take longer than a checkup of one's personal appearance. Regular checkups will serve you well if you correct what needs attention, but often we will go for weeks or months—even years—without checking up on our hearts. Why? "Men loved darkness rather than light, because their deeds were evil" (John 3:19, NKJV).

The following is a brief checkup. It will only take a few minutes:

"Pursue peace with all men, and holiness, without which no one will see the Lord: looking diligently lest anyone fall short of the grace of God; lest any root of bitterness springing up cause trouble, and by this many become defiled" (Heb. 12:14–15, NKJV).

The soul is reflected in a special kind of mirror called the Bible. It says: "If any-one is a hearer of the word and not a doer, he is like a man observing his natural face in a mirror; for he observes himself, goes away, and immediately forgets what kind of man he was. But he who looks into the perfect law of liberty and continues in it, and is not a forgetful hearer but a doer of the work, this one will be blessed in what he does" (James 1:23–25, NKJV).

Spend most of today's lesson on reflecting on your soul. Use the Bible verses printed above to examine your soul. Write your experience of checking your soul today._____

_____

_____

Is it a challenge to resolve any conflicts between you and someone else? Perhaps even the person on the other side of the bathroom wall in the morning? Does the conflict disturb you? Are you "gracious" about it? Look carefully!

Examine the Scriptures and/or your answers in today's lesson. Determine the most meaningful thought for you today. Write your thought for the day here:

_____

_____

_____

Applying what God is pointing out to you is essential. How will you apply this truth to your life today? _____

_____

Write a short prayer to God that summarizes your thoughts._____

_____

_____

_____

Did God bring to mind someone who needs to hear this truth? Who?_____

_____

Thought for the Day:

The Bible is the mirror for checking up on your soul.

◆

D A Y   F O U R

A Look in the Mirror
(Part 1)

If you glanced in a mirror and saw a pimple you would surely look more carefully. A pimple! You don't ignore a pimple! This is an emergency! You would move quickly to get rid of it.

We get the word *gracious* from the word *grace* which generally means "loving acceptance." Look carefully lest you fall short of the grace of God. Are you aware of an ungracious spirit toward a family member, a co-worker, or anyone? You still act graciously, sound gracious, but deep down inside you are not gracious. Beware. This is more serious than a pimple.

Is there a root of bitterness lurking in your heart toward the person with whom you are in open or hidden conflict? Are you making an effort to be reconciled?

Do you have bitterness toward anyone in your life? Make a list of the people in your life toward whom you are bitter. _____

_____

What are you doing to become reconciled with them? _____

_____

_____

I see many married couples who were, at one time, delighting in each other's presence, filled with admiration and appreciation for one another. Because one or both neglected their souls, they are now estranged. They have forgotten the sweet fellowship of the past, and goodwill towards one another has left their hearts. "Take heed to yourself and diligently keep yourself, lest you forget the things your eyes have seen, and lest they depart from your heart all the days of your life" (Deut. 4:9, NKJV).

When you read this verse, what did you see in the mirror that would blur your memory? _____

_____

_____

Take another quick look at the mirror that reflects your soul: "Put off all these: anger, wrath, malice, blasphemy, filthy language out of your mouth. Do not lie to one another" (Col. 3:8–9, NKJV).

What do you need to put off that is blurring your reflection? _____

_____

Also, "Put on tender mercies, kindness, humbleness of mind, meekness, longsuffering; bearing with one another, and forgiving one another . . . even as Christ forgave you, so you also must do" (Col. 3:12–13, NKJV).

Which of these attributes is a mirror to your life? _____

_____

Examine the Scriptures and/or your answers in today's lesson. Determine the most meaningful thought for you today. Write your thought for the day here:

_____

_____

_____

_____

_____

Applying what God is pointing out to you is essential. How will you apply this truth to your life today? _____

_____

_____

Write a short prayer to God that summarizes your thoughts._____

_____

_____

_____

Did God bring to mind someone who needs to hear this truth? Who?_____

_____

Thought for the Day:

An ungracious spirit will result in a broken personal relationship.

◆

D A Y   F I V E

A Look in the Mirror
(Part 2)

The Bible is a mirror that will let you know what to put off or put on. You may or may not want to know. You may or may not want to act on your reflection. You can even act like you have put off what needs putting off and put on what needs putting on when that really is not the situation under your skin.

Once I stayed in a lovely apartment with a bathroom that had mirrors on all the walls. At first I was pleased, but very quickly I was stunned. I saw views of my body that I had never seen before and I didn't like what I saw. The easy solution is to stay away from mirrors. The wise solution is to correct what needs correcting.

A couple came up to me after a speaking engagement to share with me the good news of what had happened to their marriage relationship since they both began spiritual checkups. A year earlier they had heard me speak on the subject, and at that time the wife rid herself of a load of sin that was ruining her life.

She told me how her husband had met another woman in a motel occasionally. The relationship ended. She learned about the situation when her husband and the other woman came to her and admitted they had been together.

She was livid with rage toward the other woman and refused to forgive when the woman pleaded for forgiveness. The wife nursed her rage for six years. Even though she and the other woman were now several thousand miles apart, the thought of the other woman would instantly fill her with rage.

"It was like a rope around my neck," she said. Her rage ruined her appetite, gave her pounding headaches, and often kept her awake. She knew all along that nursing her grudge against the other woman was only punishing herself. But she felt nursing an angry spirit was not evil, but pleasurable. The Bible warns, however, "If you have bitter envy and self-seeking in your hearts . . . lie [not] against the truth . . . [it] is earthly, sensual [self indulgent], demonic" (James 3:14–15, NKJV).

Take a moment to find James chapter three in your Bible. Read the passage from verse thirteen to eighteen. Isn't this a powerful passage? Based on this passage, how should the woman have responded to the other woman?

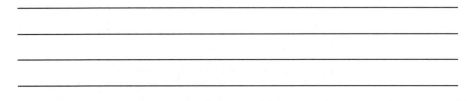

_____

_____

_____

_____

At the conference a year earlier, the wife suddenly realized that she was punishing herself because her husband and this other person had sinned. Their sin exposed her own sin. She deposited her six-year burden with the Lord; now she was free and their marriage was better than ever.

Can you imagine being at odds over something year after year in a relationship? It is amazing what a low standard of Christian life many of us will tolerate.

As you leave the bathroom in the morning, your appearance can be very different from when you went in. Likewise, we can behave differently from our feelings. We can feel isolated from others, alone in a crowd, detached from reality, uncomfortable, and ill at ease when people praise us. These conditions result because how we talk and act does not accurately reflect what is going on underneath our skin.

Man looks at the outward appearance. The Lord looks on the heart. What really matters is what the Lord sees. He sees the real person underneath our skin. That is why it is important that we deal with the negative (sin) in our lives. When we bring the sin in our life to God, He takes it away and we can actually feel under our skin just as we behave on the outside. This resting and peaceful condition of God's forgiveness gives us tremendous relief from stress and fear.

Examine the Scriptures and/or your answers in today's lesson. Determine the most meaningful thought for you today. Write your thought for the day here:

_____

_____

_____

_____

Applying what God is pointing out to you is essential. How will you apply this truth to your life today? _____

_____

_____

Write a short prayer to God that summarizes your thoughts._____

_____

_____

_____

_____

Did God bring to mind someone who needs to hear this truth? Who?_____

_____

Thought for the Day:

Man looks at the outward appearance. The Lord looks on the heart.

◆

(Optional—But Recommended!)

Bring forward your thoughts from each day:

1. _____

2. _____

3. _____

4. _____

5. _____

Bring forward your application:

1. _____
2. _____
3. _____
4. _____
5. _____

Bring forward your prayers:

1. _____
2. _____
3. _____
4. _____
5. _____

Bring forward who you shared your thoughts with:

1. _____
2. _____
3. _____
4. _____
5. _____

Thought for the Week:

As a mirror is to your face, the Bible is to your soul.

◆

U N I T   S E V E N

At What Age Is It Acceptable to Sulk When You Can't Have What You Want?

Thought Starter:

Why do adults behave childishly?

♦

Memory Verse for the Week:

Brothers, if someone is caught in a sin, you who are spiritual should restore him gently. But watch yourself, or you also may be tempted.
GALATIANS 6:1, NIV

DAY ONE

Where there are envy, strife, and divisions among you, are you not carnal and behaving like mere men?
1 CORINTHIANS 3:3, NKJV

Childish Manipulation

I was sitting alone in a living room, waiting for the man of the house to appear. Instead, a door opened and in walked a small boy. He walked over to where I was sitting and asked me some pointed questions:

"Who are you?"

"What do you want here?"

"Have you got any children?"

"I have a dog. Do you like dogs?"

"Do your children have a train like mine?"

I had my mind on the reason for my being there, so these questions were distracting me. I tried to think of some way to get his attention away from me, and all I could think of was to give him my billfold to play with.

Immediately I saw that this decision was a mistake. He began to extract my credit cards and money. I needed to redeem my billfold.

My first approach was to ask him to return it in as nice a voice as possible. "Would you please give me my billfold?"

He replied, "That's my billfold."

A simple, childlike transaction. I had no other choice but to take it away from him. In my mind, I needed to be calm, cool, and collected for my appointment, so I needed to bring this encounter with a three-year-old to a swift conclusion. I retrieved my billfold, put the credit cards and paper money in place, and pocketed the billfold. But my little friend was determined to retrieve "his" billfold. He approached me with a smile on his face and in a pleasant voice, he said, "Please, mister, can I have my billfold back?"

With such a sweet request, I felt quite mean and inconsiderate, but I replied, "No, that's my billfold."

"Can't I please have it back? Please, mister? Please, can I have it back?" he pleaded, still smiling.

I was almost persuaded to give it back to him, but I got a firmer grip on my resolve and said as gently as possible,

"No, you can't have it."

As if by magic, this nice, polite, friendly, little boy turned into someone else. His smile was gone. His eyes became slits, he stomped his feet, his little hands doubled up into fists, and in a shrill voice, he shouted, "I want my billfold!"

I said, "No!"

Then he started to cry. Tears streaming down his cheeks, he looked utterly pathetic.

He wailed, "I want my billfold."

I said, "No!"

Finally, he gave me an ugly look and turned his back on me.

He was pouting. I was getting the silent treatment. He acted as though I was non-existent.

At that point, his father showed up and the incident with the child was over. Later, I had some free time and began to relive that scene.

Can you remember the last time you received the "silent treatment?"_____

How did you respond?_____

_____

Can you remember the last time you gave the "silent treatment" to someone?

_____

Why did you take that action?_____

_____

_____

Small children have some very effective tools to get what they are after. The tools can be charming: smiling, reaching out for a hug, or sweet talk; they can also be deceptively charming: rolling their eyes, yelling, screaming, crying, or pouting. Childlike behavior can be very effective.

There are two definitions for the word *charm*. One is the expression of genuine pleasure, delight, pleasantry, and gratitude. The other is to deceive and pretend pleasure, delight, pleasantry, and gratitude to allure, entice, captivate. In either case, the behavior is the same; the motive is quite different.

I have parents approach me because their child is five years old and clearly still uses deceptive charm (as the three-year-old who approached me) to get what they are after. At what age is it no longer acceptable to use pretended pleasantry for personal gain? Would you say ten, twenty or forty years old?

Take a few minutes to answer this question: (1) At what age do you believe it is no longer acceptable to use pretended pleasantry for personal gain?

   ❑ Age 10   ❑ Age 25

   ❑ Age 15   ❑ Age 30

   ❑ Age 18   ❑ Age 35

   ❑ Age 21   ❑ Age 50

This seems a little silly, doesn't it? Why? _____

_____

_____

We were having lunch with an elderly couple. Their ten-year-old grandchild approached the table. She was all smiles and charm. With her back to Grandpa and hugging Grandma, I heard her whisper in Grandma's ear, "Grandma, can I have a dollar?"

The grandma said, "No, not now."

Then she turned around with her back to Grandma and gave Grandpa a hug and a kiss and told him she loved him. He was noticeably pleased by her attention. Then she asked him for a dollar. He gladly responded. She gave him another hug and kiss and declared her love for him; she gave Grandma a big smile, and was gone. She'd gotten her dollar.

My three-year-old friend's actions in attempting to acquire my billfold and the ten-year-old's success in charming Grandpa out of a dollar start out to be childish self-interest. But, this behavior works so well that it often is continued into adult life.

Adults are like children in many ways. Adults use many tricks to achieve people's attention or achieve a desired result from others. The use of these tricks is called deception. How would you define deception? Look the word up in a dictionary. _____

_____

_____

_____

What is the difference between deception and lying? Look up the word lie in the dictionary and compare it with deception. _____

_____

_____

Why do adults continue to use these methods of childish manipulation?

_____

_____

_____

Examine the Scriptures and/or your answers in today's lesson. Determine the most meaningful thought for you today. Write your thought for the day here:

_____

_____

_____

_____

Applying what God is pointing out to you is essential. How will you apply this truth to your life today? _____

_____

_____

Write a short prayer to God that summarizes your thoughts. _____

_____

_____

_____

_____

Did God bring to mind someone who needs to hear this truth? Who?_____

_____

Thought for the Day:
Adults often act like children.

◆

DAY TWO

Childish Behavior Isn't Just for Children

At what age is it no longer acceptable to throw a tantrum when you can't have what you want? I was lecturing a man in his forties about being a more considerate husband. He was a college graduate and a successful businessman. He nodded, approving of what I was saying, *I thought.*

Suddenly, he stood up and shouted, "I've had enough of this. I don't have to pay for this stuff. I don't need to put up with this lecture!" He wheeled around, opened the door and left, slamming the door so hard the pictures on the walls moved.

Whew!

What happened?

He had a tantrum.

Ten minutes later, the phone rang. It was he, apologizing for his behavior. This is what psychologists call *regressive behavior:* acting like a five-year-old. Why do we continue such behavior? One reason is that an individual believes it still works. Another reason is that anger and wrath are part of our sinful nature.

Can you see why adults use behavior like this man used? Look up Isaiah 53:6. There is a truth in this verse that applies to all people. What is that truth? ____

_____

_____

At what age is it acceptable to cry when you can't have what you want? A woman sits down for a meeting with me, opens her purse, and takes out a tiny handkerchief. When this happens, I can predict that this woman will cry before the hour is up. Sure enough, I will say something she doesn't like. At that point, an amazing thing happens: She will produce one tear from each eye. Not two tears, but one. This is her signal for me to back away from the subject we are on, or perhaps to let me know that I have said something she doesn't like. It is remarkable how long a tear can be suspended in the corner of her eye, but eventually it will trickle down her cheek. At that point she will whisk it away with a practiced hand.

Let me assure you that I am not referring to tears of sorrow or grief or loneliness or real guilt. I refer to the use of tears as a tool to manipulate others so one can get his or her own way. Why do people continue such behavior into adult life? Because it has worked successfully in the past. Another reason is that selfishness is part of our sinful nature.

At what age is it acceptable to pout when you can't have what you want? I talked with a couple struggling with both temper tantrums and pouting. Their large home was the scene of much conflict. He wished she were more orderly; she wished he were less rigid. One day he flew into a rage over her closet, demanding that she get it organized. Then he slammed the door, got into his car, and took off, spinning the wheels of his car as he went.

The silence continued for three days. She pouted in response to his tantrum. She would teach him not to yell at her and make demands she refused to meet. This interaction between them had been going on for many years.

What advice would you give this couple? _____

_____

_____

Why do adults sulk when they can't have what they want? Because it worked in the past and it still works for them. Another reason is that anger, rebellion, and selfishness are part of our sinful nature.

How do you respond when someone sulks? Check all that apply.
- ☐ I ignore the person.
- ☐ I feel sorry for the person and I try to console him/her.
- ☐ I get mad at the person and let them know that I am mad.
- ☐ I treat them like a child because that is how he/she is acting.
- ☐ I avoid them because I do not want a relationship with that kind of person.

Paul wrote to some young Christians that he could not treat them as grown-up spiritual people. He pointed out that they were missing out on the happiness that comes with living lives when Christ is in control. They were missing personality qualities such as "love, joy, peace, longsuffering, kindness, goodness, faithfulness, gentleness, and self-control" (Gal. 5:22, NKJV).

According to the Bible, the only way to actually acquire these qualities as part of your being is to recognize that you don't have them unless God gives them to you. Your part is to allow the Holy Spirit to give you something you don't have.

Examine the Scriptures and/or your answers in today's lesson. Determine the most meaningful thought for you today. Write your thought for the day here:

_____

_____

_____

_____

Applying what God is pointing out to you is essential. How will you apply this truth to your life today? _____

_____

_____

Write a short prayer to God that summarizes your thoughts._____

_____

_____

_____

_____

Did God bring to mind someone who needs to hear this truth? Who?_____

_____

Thought for the Day:

Adults continue unacceptable behavior because it has worked in the past and is part of our sinful nature.

◆

D A Y   T H R E E

Carnality

Paul used the word *carnal*. We don't see or hear this word used today. Some modern translations say "worldly," one "babes," another "fleshly." Paul said: "Where there are envy, strife, and divisions among you, are you not carnal and behaving like mere men?" (1 Cor. 3:3, NKJV).

Envy, strife, and divisiveness hinder learning and appreciation of others. The apostle Paul calls them "mere men," rather than "spiritual men."

During a recent series of evangelistic meetings, a man with a beautiful singing voice invited Christ to take control of his life. He began attending a church. They soon discovered his fine voice and called on him to sing for some of the church services. Ironically, I had a counselee with a good voice who attended the same church. He was doing the male solo work until this new believer with the better voice came along. They shared vocal responsibilities. My counselee discovered envy and strife in his heart; he could not enjoy the beauty of this new convert's voice. He deeply resented the music director's decision to use the new singer. Several people who knew the situation sided with the music director. There was carnality, envy, strife, and division in my counselee's heart. There was no point in talking about spiritual life with him. He needed to be reminded of the most basic principles of the Christian life. This talented, successful man needed to be approached as if he were a child who knew nothing about the Lord.

As Paul put it: "I fed you with milk and not with solid food; for until now you were not able to receive it" (1 Cor. 3:2, NKJV).

Once Jesus told His disciples, "I have yet many things to say unto you, but ye cannot bear them now" (John 16:12, KJV).

Isaiah said to his people: "Whom shall he teach knowledge? and whom shall he make to understand doctrine? them that are weaned from the milk, and drawn from the breasts. For precept must be upon precept, precept upon precept; line upon line, line upon line; here a little, and there a little" (Isa. 28:9–10, KJV).

As children often do, my counselee struggled for a while; he wanted his singing position back. There were some tantrums, some weeping, some pouting. Finally, there was some repenting or changing of his mind. Today, he is being blessed by the fine singing voice of his vocal partner. Besides, he is chewing on some solid food.

"If we live in the Spirit, let us also walk in the Spirit" (Gal. 5:25, NKJV). In order to develop spiritually, we must recognize any carnality or childish, sinful behavior that continues on into adult life. Once the condition is discovered, only God can cure the situation. He alone can clean our hearts from envy, strife, divisions, pouting, temper tantrums, and deceptive manipulation of others. Then we can move on to the meat of the Christian life.

As Paul said, "And I, brethren, could not speak to you as to spiritual people but as to carnal, as to babes in Christ. I fed you with milk and not with solid food; for until now you were not able to receive it, and even now you are still not able; for you are still carnal. For where there are envy, strife, and divisions among you, are you not carnal and behaving like mere men?" (1 Cor. 3:1–3, NKJV).

Examine the Scriptures and/or your answers in today's lesson. Determine the most meaningful thought for you today. Write your thought for the day here:

_____

_____

_____

Applying what God is pointing out to you is essential. How will you apply this truth to your life today? _____

_____

Write a short prayer to God that summarizes your thoughts. _____

_____

_____

_____

_____

Did God bring to mind someone who needs to hear this truth? Who?_____

_____

Thought for the Day:
Carnality keeps you from understanding spiritual things.

◆

DAY FOUR

[Jesus said,] "Take heed to yourselves. If your brother sins against you, rebuke him; and if he repents, forgive him. And if he sins against you seven times in a day, and seven times in a day returns to you, saying, 'I repent,' you shall forgive him." And the apostles said to the Lord, "Increase our faith."

LUKE 17:3-5, NKJV

A Victim of Your Own Behavior

Webster defines *forgive* as, "to grant free pardon, cease to feel resentment against."

What are you to do when you must work together with someone who repeats undesirable behavior over and over again, often deliberately and sadistically? This was my question one summer when I was working with the North American Indian Mission along the spectacular coast of British Columbia. Each year the mission sponsored a summer program, placing college students on many of the beautiful islands scattered along the coast line. The mission would assign a team of four to eight college students to an island for a month. Their job was to make friends with the native Indian islanders, to develop a recreation program for the children and an arts and crafts program for the adults, and to encourage them to attend mission meetings and Bible studies.

The mission had a large ship which cruised up the coast from Vancouver to the southern tip of Alaska. Several seaplanes would regularly meet the ship and fly the teams of students to their assigned islands. My job was to help supervise the teams of students. With a pilot and seaplane I flew from island to island to see how the work was progressing.

I had no experience with seaplanes, but I found it a thrilling experience to take off and to land on the water. After my first landing at one of the islands, the pilot asked me to jump out on the dock and hold the rope which was tied to the pontoon of the plane. Glad to be of help, I stood rope in hand under the wing. When the pilot jumped out of the plane and onto the pontoon, the wing came down and struck me in the head. Boom! I saw stars! The pilot was apologetic, "I'm sorry." I replied, "That's okay."

I walked up to the primitive little village where a team of college students were eager to share with me all the unexpected challenges that had arisen. The little kids were hard to manage. They swore. They had lice in their hair. After advising, encouraging, and praying with the team, I returned to the plane.

I made note that these students would need frequent visits to encourage them and to remind them to depend on the Lord daily for grace, love, patience, and wisdom.

The pilot once again asked me to hold the rope while he got into the plane. I was glad to oblige. He jumped on the pontoon. The wing came down and smacked me in the head. Whack! Again I saw stars!

He said, "I'm so sorry." I said, "That's okay."

My head was somewhat sore, but I ignored it. There was far too much excitement in taking off over the water and rugged landscape. What was a little bump on the head compared to working with such devoted students and these needy Indian children.

As we flew to the next island, I was mildly annoyed at the pilot. My head throbbed, but the beautiful scenery and the three-foot waves which met us at our next landing absorbed my attention.

The pilot asked me to hop out on the dock and hold the rope while he secured the plane. Again I was happy to oblige. Again I felt useful. I was caught off guard when the wing came down on my head: Bang!

The pilot said, "So sorry." I said, "That's okay."

I know what you are thinking. Why didn't I just get out from under that wing? The excitement of the landings and launchings, the lovely views and my observations of the Indian culture all added up to forgetting to look out for my head.

On the way up to see the students, I began to wonder how sorry the pilot really was. This was no longer okay! I thought that if this happens again, I will throw him into the ocean!

When we arrived at the village the students told me that they could not get along with each other. One of the fellows was very messy. He had promised his friends that he would change, but he didn't. I told them to be more forgiving of one another.

The pilot and I walk down to the dock. He asked me to hold the rope while he got into the plane. I was glad to comply. The pilot jumps on the pontoon, the wing came down, and I was nowhere near it. I gloated to myself, "Ah, ha! You missed me!"

As we flew along, I rubbed my head and nursed my mean, nasty thoughts; I half grumbled and half prayed for help. Then it hit me like the wing of a seaplane. I had visited teams of students that had to live with circumstances beyond their control. I advised the students to look to God for love, grace, and peace in their difficulties. They had to be more loving and more forgiving of one another.

In the midst of my anger I remembered the following scripture: "Take heed to yourselves. If your brother sins against you, rebuke him; and if he repents, forgive him. And if he sins against you seven times in a day, and seven times in a day returns to you, saying, 'I repent,' you shall forgive him. And the apostles said to the Lord, "Increase our faith" (Luke 17:3–5, NKJV).

I thought to myself, I'm with the apostles. If I am to forgive this character and like it, then something special must happen to me now.

Can you think of a particular incident or accident that consumed your thinking for an entire day? Write it down _____

_____

_____

Why did this incident or accident consume your thinking?_____

_____

How did you deal with it?_____

_____

_____

Isn't it amazing how our own reaction to a particular situation can so consume us that we forget about God and what He wants to do in our lives to teach us right in the middle of what is happening? Many times our thoughts are consumed because we put our eyes on other peoples' behavior and not on what Christ would desire of us in that situation. How do you respond to this question and statement?_____

_____

_____

There I was sitting beside a pilot who was also sacrificially serving the Lord. Yes, I was angry and resentful toward him. And I had said nothing. I argued with myself: What about this pilot? I don't think he's the least bit sorry! So what? If he isn't going to change, why not get out from under the wing? Not a bad idea! But is it fair for him to do this three times?

Enough of this kind of thinking, I said to myself. I had struck out on two counts. Why not admit it? First, my heart needed to be cleansed and renewed; my attitude was indefensible! Second, I failed to confront the pilot. Such behavior was clearly a violation of what Jesus taught.

I admitted to God that my attitude was lousy and that I had failed to communicate with the pilot. I asked Him to forgive me, to cleanse me, and to renew my spirit. The Lord heard my prayer and my heart was changed right there in that plane. I was the victim of my own behavior.

We approached another island where we would spend the night. The landing was smooth. The pilot asked me to jump on the dock and hold the rope. I was only too glad to comply. I was a wise, knowledgeable veteran. The pilot crawled out of the plane and, as always, jumped on the pontoon. The wing came down and disturbed only air; Brandt's head was not under the wing!

That night under the stars, as we sat around a campfire, I told the pilot about my struggle. Jesus says to rebuke someone who sins against you. I assumed I should be gracious about it. "You kept saying you were sorry," I reminded him.

"What I meant was, 'I'm sorry if you're too dumb to get out from under the wing,'" he replied, holding his sides with laughter.

This incident started my thinking. Was he serious? Did he mean that he deliberately jumped on the pontoon, knowing that I stood under the wing and would receive a whack on the head? Was this a typical bush pilot joke that they all played on newcomers? Perhaps he had adopted a popular view that says you learn best by taking the consequences for misbehaving. But shouldn't he at least have instructed me to get out from under the wing when he jumps on the pontoon? Our verse says: "If your brother sins against you, rebuke him; and if he repents, forgive him" (Luke 17:34, NKJV).

How often are you to forgive those who sin against you?

❑ Once a day.
❑ Three times a day.
❑ Twenty times a day.
❑ As many times as he/she sins against you.

Did that mean that I should chew him out? Vent my wrath on him? What if he said he had repented but continued his unacceptable behavior?

Another verse will shed some light on these questions: "Brethren, if a man is overtaken in any trespass, you who are spiritual restore such a one in a spirit of gentleness, considering yourself lest you also be tempted" (Gal. 6:1, NKJV).

This verse tells me that if anyone mistreats me, I need to first examine my own heart. I need to be "spiritual" before I approach the other person. What is "spiritual"? "The fruit of the Spirit is love, joy, peace, longsuffering, kindness, goodness, faithfulness, gentleness, self-control" (Gal. 5:22–23, NKJV).

If I am not spiritual, I need to straighten myself out before I approach the other person.

If I qualify, I need to rebuke him; that is, I need to point out the offensive or unacceptable behavior to my brother. His response shouldn't affect my spirit because my spirit is between God and me.

What about the other person's behavior? If he repents, forgive him, that is, to grant free pardon and cease to feel resentment against him.

In this instance he did repent. He agreed to warn me when he was about to jump on the pontoon. Obviously, I needed to keep on being "spiritual." His present or future conduct didn't dictate the condition of my heart.

In the future, I could be more alert. I could accept his way of doing things. When he is around the plane, I could be sure not to be under the wing. Occasionally I could remind him to let me know when he was about to jump on the pontoon. Otherwise, I would allow myself to become the victim of my own behavior or lack of behavior.

Examine the Scriptures and/or your answers in today's lesson. Determine the most meaningful thought for you today. Write your thought for the day here:

_____

_____

_____

Applying what God is pointing out to you is essential. How will you apply this truth to your life today? _____

_____

_____

_____

Write a short prayer to God that summarizes your thoughts._____

_____

_____

_____

Did God bring to mind someone who needs to hear this truth? Who?_____

_____

Thoughts for the Day:

It is easy to become distressed or disappointed by people's actions and behaviors.

———

A spirit of forgiveness brings peace to your mind.

◆

DAY FIVE

Rebuke and Forgive

Suppose someone is repentant and still repeats undesirable behavior over and over. Our verse says to rebuke and forgive.

I found myself in this situation with my wife, Jo. Shortly after saying our marriage vows, we learned that some adjustments were necessary.

I was driving, and Jo was sitting next to me when she said, "Henry, would you please not drive so closely to the car in front of us?"

I proceeded to defend my driving style and driving record, "Look, I haven't had an accident in years and I am in better passing position when I am close to the next car." She insisted that I was driving too close. We were clearly annoyed at each other.

Finally I saw the light. How selfish of me to ignore her request and not make driving with me more relaxing for her. I agreed to open the distance between our car and the one we were following. But I learned that driving habits are not easily changed. I would unthinkingly lapse into my old habits. Often I would remind myself; if I didn't, Jo surely would. There were some trips when I needed to repent seven times in a day. After weeks of catching myself and Jo rebuking me, I developed the habit of staying the proper distance from the car in front of me. Occasionally, I need to correct and "walk in the Spirit." She needs to rebuke and forgive.

Read Matthew 5:22-24. How do these verses ask a person to mend a hurt relationship?

☐ Ignore the wrong and hope things get better.
☐ Continue your worship to the Lord.
☐ Make things right with your friend and then worship the Lord.
☐ Take your friend to court.

What other thoughts came to your mind when you read these verses? _____

_____

_____

_____

We had another adjustment to make. Jo had a habit of taking off her glasses and laying them on her lap, a table, a car seat, or any other handy place. They would slide off her lap and disappear, or she would forget where she left them. She was constantly looking for them.

This was unacceptable to me. I felt something simple could be done to solve the problem. She reluctantly agreed to put them in her purse when she took them off when she was away from home. At home, there were two designated places for them. If I saw her put them down anywhere else, I would remind her on the spot. For a while it was a case of reminding her many times every day. Her response wasn't very friendly, and neither was my response to her response. We both had to repent of our bad attitudes. But the "rebuke-repent" process worked. It quickly became apparent that knowing where her glasses were was worth the effort on both of our parts.

These adjustments made it clear that we both needed to walk "in the Spirit" and we need to maintain a "rebuke-repent" process to deal with occasional lapses.

I met with a man who came to see me regarding his wife. He had married a door slammer. She would slam the car door as hard as she could. She'd slam the front door, the kitchen cupboard doors, the bedroom doors, the bathroom door, and any other door she needed to close. He would wince whenever she approached a door. He could hardly stand it any more.

"Have you talked to her about it?" I asked.

"No, we have only been married a few months. If I criticize her it may hurt her self-image. I am trying to encourage her."

I called his attention to Galatians 6:1. No need to be critical. The Lord will help him to be gentle. There is no way for her to know what is in his mind if he doesn't tell her.

When he asked her to close the doors more gently, she was quite willing to comply. She had no idea that this behavior troubled him; he was greatly relieved. She then got up out of her chair and went to the bedroom and slammed the door. She was truly willing to change, but slamming doors was so much of a habit she did it without thinking. She actually needed to repent seven times a day, and he needed to forgive her just as often. But with two of them working together, she changed her behavior in a few weeks. It took two spiritual people who worked together to solve a problem.

What is your pet peeve? _____

_____

_____

Do you have a favorite pet peeve you want to keep? _____

_____

How do you deal with it? _____

_____

_____

How often do you need to deal with your unacceptable behavior? Until you stop!

What do you do about unacceptable behavior that may be repeated seven times in a day? *First, you walk in the Spirit.* It is a fallacy to blame someone else's behavior for your anger or resentment. This is a sin. Your spirit involves God and you. *Second, there needs to be a change of behavior.* You need to rebuke, that is, describe the unacceptable behavior. *Third, you need to deal with the person's response.* If there is repentance, you forgive. If there is improvement, you praise. But what if there is no change? What then?

What should your response be if someone says they are sorry, but repeats the same behavior day in and day out? You may need to conclude that "I am sorry" is meaningless. What you do about it depends on the relationship. Are you dealing with a child, a parent, your partner, a friend, an employee? Certainly, you need to walk in the Spirit. *Fourth, depending on the relationship, you may need to reward, praise, punish, remind, train or even fire someone.*

List the four steps to dealing with unacceptable behavior that is directed toward you.

1. _____
2. _____
3. _____
4. _____

In my case, I simply needed to get out from under the wing. My assignment to hold a rope provided me with some insight into my own heart and the chance to learn a new lesson about communication and forgiveness (and how to avoid a bump on the head!)

Examine the Scriptures and/or your answers in today's lesson. Determine the most meaningful thought for you today. Write your thought for the day here:

_____

_____

_____

_____

Applying what God is pointing out to you is essential. How will you apply this truth to your life today? _____

_____

_____

Write a short prayer to God that summarizes your thoughts._____

_____

_____

_____

_____

Did God bring to mind someone who needs to hear this truth? Who?_____

_____

Thought for the Day:

Rebuking and forgiving should only be done when controlled by the Spirit.

♦

(Optional—But Recommended!)

Bring forward your thoughts from each day:

1. _____
2. _____
3. _____
4. _____
5. _____

Bring forward your application:

1. _____
2. _____
3. _____
4. _____
5. _____

Bring forward your prayers:

1. _____
2. _____
3. _____
4. _____
5. _____

Bring forward who you shared your thoughts with:

1. _____
2. _____
3. _____
4. _____
5. _____

Thought for the Week:

Do not allow yourself to become the victim of your own behavior.

◆

UNIT EIGHT

I Need to Forgive Those Soldiers

Thought Starter:

Has a grudge ever helped you?

◆

Memory Verse for the Week:

Be gentle and ready to forgive; never hold grudges. Remember, the Lord forgave you, so you must forgive others.
COLOSSIANS 3:13, TLB

DAY ONE

Potential Power

A bloody civil war raged in Uganda. There were shortages of food, water, vehicles, gasoline, and clothing. The roads had potholes the size of a car. Everywhere we looked there were ugly war machines: tanks, trucks, artillery. We had to pass through frequent checkpoints manned by armed teenaged soldiers. We were stopped twelve times while driving the twenty-five miles from the Entebbe airport to the capital city of Kampala. Each checkpoint made us open our bags for inspection.

The next day, we were to travel to the city of Goma, where I was scheduled to address a meeting. Sam, my driver, had been scouring in vain to find some gasoline for our vehicle. We were three hours late when Sam finally came to me to say he found some gas for $30 per gallon. We needed fifteen gallons or $450 worth.

I questioned our going. Who would wait for a foreign speaker who is three hours late? Sam convinced me we should go. It was a slow, bumpy ride, and there were more roadblocks manned by unfriendly soldiers. We arrived at the meeting place which was packed with people. It was so hot and humid that the air in the room was almost unbearable.

I sat on the platform, looking out at the audience. I knew most of them were hungry. They were shabbily dressed and I knew no one in this audience had stood in front of a closet packed full of clothes and wondered what to wear. What could I say to these people when I had never wondered what I would eat or wear? I knew that many of them had suffered the death of a family member. Many of their families were scattered, some having fled into the forest to avoid being mowed down by hostile gunfire. I prayed silently, "Lord, I don't know what to say to these people. God, you have to help me."

The only thought that came to me was: "But the fruit of the Spirit is love, joy, peace, long-suffering, kindness, goodness, faithfulness, gentleness, self-control. Against such there is no law" (Gal. 5:22–23, NKJV).

Is it realistic to expect them to be filled with the Spirit?_____

_____

If you had been with these people during this traumatic time, what would you have said to them?_____

_____

_____

For anyone to be receptive to Scripture like this requires a miracle!

I told them I believed that each one of them could have all they wanted of a free gift. The gift was the fruit of the Spirit. It was freely available to my people, and I believed it was also available to them.

After the meeting, a raggedly dressed man approached me. He said I seemed uncertain about my message. He reassured me that the fruit of the Spirit was available in Uganda, but I had left an important condition out of my message. He asked me if I would take the time to come to his home. He would like to tell me his story.

As we walked down a dusty road in the intense heat, he pointed to a large house, with perhaps five or six bedrooms, up in the hills. "That was my house," he said, "but Idi Amin's soldiers came one day and took it as headquarters for his army. My family had to flee and today they are in the forest. I had a Mercedes-Benz parked in front of my clothing store. One day the soldiers came and took my car. Then they took my store."

We had been walking on this dusty road lined with mud-walled huts with thatched roofs. We came to one and he indicated that this was where he lived. We entered it: one dark room, dirt floor, and a box on the floor. He motioned me to sit on the box. He sat on the other end of it and continued his story.

"I would sit in my chair and work myself into a frenzy over the soldiers who took my car, my business, my house, and scattered my family. I was consumed with hatred, bitterness, and anger.

"When I was forced to leave my house, I took along a chair. I had a cow, also, which needed some fly spray. I traded my chair for the fly spray, but my cow died. I also had a goat and traded my goat for some seeds to plant a garden. But it didn't rain, so my garden failed. Now I have no car, no business, no house, no family, no chair, no cow, no goat, no garden.

"One day, as I sat on this box and rehearsed all of this, I thought I would burst with hatred and animosity. A man came to my door in the middle of this situation. He said he was a missionary and had come to tell me that God loved me. That's all I heard. 'God loves me?' I exploded: 'Do you know what has happened to me?'

"In a rage, I picked that man up and threw him out of my house. God loves me! I was so mad I could hardly contain myself! To my surprise, the man got up and came back in. I was startled at his boldness. He said he had come to tell me about Jesus and would like to continue. He told me, 'God loves you so much that He gave His own Son to die for you. If you ask Him, He will come into your life and change your heart.'

How wise was it for the missionary to talk to the man about accepting Christ at this point?_____

Shouldn't the man have waited for a better time to witness? Why or why not?

_____

_____

"At that moment I was so furious I hardly knew what to do with myself. Then suddenly, what this man said gave me some hope. I needed something, so I asked Jesus to come into my life right then. He did."

Examine the Scriptures and/or your answers in today's lesson. Determine the most meaningful thought for you today. Write your thought for the day here:

_____

_____

_____

_____

Applying what God is pointing out to you is essential. How will you apply this truth to your life today? _____

_____

_____

Write a short prayer to God that summarizes your thoughts._____

_____

_____

_____

Did God bring to mind someone who needs to hear this truth? Who?_____

_____

Thought for the Day:

What do you think about this statement: Receiving Christ does not solve any of your problems.

◆

D A Y   T W O

Love and Forgiveness

Now I come to the part of my story that has to do with your message. I told you that something was missing.

"When I asked Jesus to come into my life, I could still see my home occupied by soldiers, my Mercedes-Benz being driven by soldiers, my business ruined, my family scattered, without a garden, and wondering how to survive. My heart was still filled with animosity toward those soldiers. My new friend read me a Bible verse intended for children of God: "For if you forgive men their trespasses, your heavenly Father will also forgive you. But if you do not forgive men their trespasses, neither will your Father forgive your trespasses" (Matt. 6:14–15, NKJV).

"A shaft of light into utter darkness! I needed to forgive those soldiers. I needed to love them. Suddenly I wanted to love them. I opened my heart and poured out all the hate and anger and bitterness that I had stored up there. All I wanted was the fruit of the Spirit in my heart.

"You are right," he said. "We can have all we want for free. But you must meet God's terms. You must forgive men their trespasses."

My new friend said he was the richest man in Uganda. He had been released from the unbearable load of sin (hate, anger, bitterness) and now was basking in the unlimited wealth of the fruit of the Spirit. He reminded me that God is the source of the fruit of the Spirit. As we parted, I promised him that I would share his story with others.

As I walked away, I remembered a man who had never paid me back some money I had lent him. I had nursed a grudge against him for a long time. (Webster's defines a grudge as a "cherished ill will with deep resentment at a real or imagined slight.") I, too, had to release that grudge; I did after a struggle similar to my new friend's struggle. The man still owed me the money, but what a difference to love a debtor instead of hating him.

My new friend faced greater problems than most of us can imagine. How foolish it was to add the pain resulting from hate, anger, and bitterness when he could change them for peace, joy, love, kindness, and forgiveness.

I can be just as angry over my little problems as my friend could be over his big ones. The fact that a man did not pay me back my money did not determine what was in my heart. His decision only revealed the condition of my heart. The money issue is between the man and me. The condition of my heart is between God and me.

I will never forget the man from Uganda who took the time to minister to me. In order for any of us to experience the fruit of the Spirit, we must let go of our pet grudges. For him it meant to forgive those unnamed soldiers. For me it was someone who failed to repay a debt owed to me.

Many people who come to me for help hold long-standing grudges. Years ago I naively thought that it would be music to their ears to hear that they could let them go and be released from the ill will and animosity that gripped their hearts. I have learned that for many people, the older a grudge (or a pet peeve) gets, the more precious it becomes, like a family heirloom. A person can carefully nurture a grudge. It may be toward someone several thousand miles away. You can recall such a grudge when you have an odd moment to reminisce, work yourself into a frenzy, then carefully put it aside until you have another off moment. To give up that grudge would be a sacrifice rather than release.

Remember, God loves us and will allow circumstances to come into our lives in order to show us what is in our hearts. Jesus said, "Love your enemies, bless those who curse you, do good to those who hate you, and pray for those who spitefully use you and persecute you" (Matt. 5:44, NKJV).

At another conference, in Zimbabwe, I told the audience the story of the Ugandan businessman who had lost everything when Idi Amin's soldiers seized his possessions and his family had to flee to the forests. This businessman had peace in his heart only after he forgave the soldiers.

Tomorrow you will read an amazing story of a couple who responded to the testimony of this businessman.

Examine the Scriptures and/or your answers in today's lesson. Determine the most meaningful thought for you today. Write your thought for the day here:

_____

_____

_____

_____

Applying what God is pointing out to you is essential. How will you apply this truth to your life today? _____

_____

_____

Write a short prayer to God that summarizes your thoughts._____

_____

_____

_____

_____

Did God bring to mind someone who needs to hear this truth? Who?_____

_____

Thoughts for the Day:

The circumstances that come into our lives will show us what is in our hearts.

———

Receiving Christ makes the fruit of the Spirit available to you.

♦

DAY THREE

How Can I Forgive?

After my morning address, I received a note requesting a private meeting. To my surprise, I found myself sitting across from a couple from Uganda who had been urged by some friends to attend this conference. Deeply disturbed by a tragedy in their own lives, the couple had listened intently to the story of my Ugandan friend.

As they sat before me, they told me how they had struggled to keep their business going in spite of the turbulence of Uganda's last twenty years.

Then one day during the bloody reign of Idi Amin, they received a note stating their twenty-six-year-old son had been kidnapped and was being held for ransom. The parents did nothing for a few days, and then received a note threatening that their son would be killed if they did not pay the ransom.

The couple sought legal advice and consulted with the proper government authorities. They were advised to resist payment. Then came another note. This was the final warning. If payment was not made immediately, their son would be tortured and killed. As they agonized over what to do, they received a note stating that their son was dead. Grief-stricken, the father tried to locate the body.

Finally he found someone who, for a price, would lead him to his son's body. When he arrived at the appointed place late one night, he was seized by a group of soldiers and taken to a prison. In the same cell that had held his son, they stripped him to the waist and made him face a wall. With a whip made of leather strips, they cut his back to ribbons. They loaded him into the back of a pickup truck and dropped him off on a street corner. They shouted at him that if he ever tried to locate his son again, he would be killed.

Two years had passed. The couple had suffered bitter, deep hatred toward unknown soldiers who murdered their son and beat the father until he was unable to lie on his back for two months. They could no longer enjoy success in business, a spacious home in the country, and a happy family life. Now each day was filled with sorrow, hatred, and thoughts of revenge. The story of the Ugandan businessman had disturbed them; they wanted to know if I believed they were wrong to treasure their misery and keep their hatred alive. It seemed to them that resentment was normal and proper. To forgive the soldiers seemed to them to be inappropriate and disloyal to the memory of their son.

Suppose this couple asked you to help them with their situation. How would you help them? What would you say? _____

_____

_____

_____

Where do you turn to for wisdom in a situation like this? _____

_____

_____

_____

What could I say? Theirs was a tragic story. Surely they had the option to choose their own approach to the cruel, heartless event that had clouded their lives. The problem was so far removed from my own life experiences that it seemed almost from another world. I required more wisdom than I possessed. "God, help me," I quietly prayed.

We sat in silence in a dimly lit room. I couldn't think of anything to say to the dear couple. The woman's eyes were filled with tears. The gentleman sat with his elbows on his knees and both hands covering his face. The wife whispered, "It would be a relief to put this behind us and get on with the future." "Yes, it would," he replied. "Can you help us?"

You can take your time in responding to a difficult question. Do you agree? Why?_____

_____

_____

_____

How could I help? I leaned back in my chair and thought to myself, "What would the Ugandan businessman who had lost everything say to them right now? I believe he would have said: "Let all bitterness, wrath, anger, clamor, and evil speaking be put away from you, with all malice. And be kind to one another, tenderhearted, forgiving one another, just as God in Christ forgave you" (Eph. 4:31–32, NKJV).

Murder and merciless beatings are heinous deeds. Many friends and associates assured them that revenge, anger, and hatred were natural responses. To think of being kind and tenderhearted and forgiving was beyond consideration.

Would God want them to change their heart attitudes? _____

As the three of us struggled in that dark room in Zimbabwe, it seemed to me that there was another presence in the room. God was there telling me to gently urge this dear couple to let go of their hostile spirit and let Him cleanse their hearts. He would give them a kind, tender, forgiving spirit. Jesus would say: "But I say to you, love your enemies, bless those who curse you, do good to those who hate you, and pray for those who spitefully use you and persecute you" (Matt. 5:44, NKJV).

I suggested that they needed to pray for such a change of heart, and after a long silence, the man said in a trembling voice, "I am ready." His wife said, "So am I."

How long does it take the Lord to heal a situation like this when the person is ready? _____

_____

The three of us knelt by the bed in that quiet room. I have never heard such moving prayers. We stood up and embraced each other with tears of supernatural joy streaming down our cheeks.

The next day the man and his wife stood before the entire gathering. He told the group that he and his wife were leaving a heavy burden behind and looking forward to a new life in the future. I knew what he meant.

God's children have full access to the limitless supply of the fruit of His Spirit: love, joy, peace, longsuffering, kindness, goodness, faithfulness, gentleness, and self-control. Isn't it odd, therefore, that we should ever choose hatred, resentment, or anger, not over the great tragedies of life, but more often, over the small grievances of daily living?

Inevitably, my response is involved in a deed that needs my forgiveness. This response forces me into the need for personal examination. If there is anger, hatred, the desire for revenge, or physical attack, then I must deal *with me* before I can deal with the offense. I can get so preoccupied with the offense, I fail to recognize my own need. Jesus once advised a multitude: "Why do you look at the speck in your brother's eye, but do not consider the plank in your own eye? . . . Hypocrite! First remove the plank from your own eye, and then you will see clearly to remove the speck from your brother's eye" (Matt. 7:3, 5, NKJV).

To forgive and be forgiven go hand in hand. Therefore, when someone trespasses against us, we usually must deal with our own sins as well as with the other person.

But people want to know when it is acceptable not to forgive. We are confronted on all sides with stories of physical abuse, sexual abuse, rape, unfaithfulness, stealing, suffering, swindling. The list is long. Is no one entitled to withhold forgiveness? Why should we forgive such treatment? The answer is clear.

The Ugandan couple experienced a miraculous cure when they were released from anger and bitterness. Forgiveness freed them from the non-productive and destructive emotions which chained them and enslaved them to the object of their anger. They found that forgiveness was the foundation of good mental health.

"These things have I spoken to you, that in Me you may have peace. In the world you will have tribulation; but be of good cheer, I have overcome the world" (John 16:33, NKJV).

Examine the Scriptures and/or your answers in today's lesson. Determine the most meaningful thought for you today. Write your thought for the day here:

_____

_____

_____

Applying what God is pointing out to you is essential. How will you apply this truth to your life today? _____

_____

_____

Write a short prayer to God that summarizes your thoughts._____

_____

_____

_____

_____

Did God bring to mind someone who needs to hear this truth? Who?_____

_____

Thought for the Day:
Forgiving quiets your own heart.

♦

DAY FOUR

I Hate Pain!

This lesson moves from how to forgive to how to deal with physical pain.

"This day is sacred to our Lord. Do not grieve, for the joy of the LORD is your strength."
NEHEMIAH 8:10, NIV

This is the day which the Lord has made; we will rejoice and be glad in it.
PSALMS 118:24, NKJV

Several years ago I had some difficulty digesting one of my wife's typical, sumptuous, delicious Christmas dinners. The discomfort lasted several days and a physician neighbor urged me to go to the hospital the next morning for a blood test.

A short time after the examination, he came into the waiting room and told me my appendix had to come out immediately. My reply was: "Hey, let's cool it and think it over for a few days. I know you need the work, but let's slow down here." He assured me that he was serious. I was to go at once to a hospital room, and he would operate as soon as I could be prepared for surgery. Prior to this I had only been hospitalized for two days to give an injured knee some rest.

The next thing I knew I awoke from the effects of the anesthesia. For two days my total attention was focused on me and my excruciating, horrible, unendurable pain! The pain was so bad that I'd consider carefully before even moving a hand! All the muscles in my body would become tense, anticipating another knife-stabbing pain.

The first day after surgery, a nurse insisted that I get out of bed and take a few steps. "You are kidding," I said, "There is no way you'll get me to do that!"

Unyielding, she firmly made me get up. The pain was incredible. A cold sweat all over my body added to my amazing, unbelievable discomfort. I would cringe with every move. To take one more step seemed inconceivable. She claimed that to move around was a short-cut to healing and to the elimination of future extended pain. But returning to my bed was beyond consideration. I told the nurse that I would just remain standing in the middle of the room if it was okay with her. Remaining firm, she forced me back into bed. Exhausted, all I could concentrate on was my painful body bathed in sweat. All I wanted was a pill to rescue me from my misery.

During the second night, when darkness enveloped the room, it was a lonely, forsaken place indeed. I'm sure there were no audible voices in that room, and I have no idea what time it was, but it was as though I heard a voice that said: "Why do you lay there suffering alone when I laid down my life to be with you, to give you my peace and joy and comfort?"

For the first time in two days, my mind was focused on something other than my own misery.

As I lay there in the hospital bed, I began thinking that for more than a quarter of a century I had traveled the world, telling people about Jesus. I had taught people that He gave His life so that He could come into our lives and be with us, that He promised to comfort us, and that He promised to give us peace and joy. I have taught this all these years, and now, here I lay, all alone, bathed in sweat, my muscles in knots, dreading every new second of my miserable life. Surely this is not peace or joy. This is not fellowship with the Lord.

It hit me: for two days and a night I had not given a thought toward the Lord. I had not even considered that peace and joy were possible with the presence of this pain I felt. I had been told that the discomfort would last for two weeks. Surely comfort and peace meant the absence of pain; they had nothing to do with God! I was shocked at my own thinking!

Why was he two days late in coming to God? _____

_____

_____

The details of a crisis can short-circuit your dependence on God and take up all your attention.

Why was I two days late in coming to God? Well, this was the first physically painful experience in my life that I couldn't handle. I never related pain with peace because I had never had to in the past. I might have hit my finger with a hammer or had a sore knee, but that was the worst that had happened to me physically.

I like Billy Graham's definition of joy:

Joy is not gush: joy is not jolliness.
Joy is simply perfect acquiescence in God's will,
because the soul delights itself in God.[1]

I began to pray, "Lord, I'm sorry I've turned my back on You. I've assumed that comfort and peace depended on finding a painless position in bed or swallowing a pill. Forgive me, Lord. I thought I was dependent on You, but here I am trying to be self-sufficient. If your Word is true, then I repent. Comfort me. Restore Your peace and joy."

I was amazed that I felt my muscles relax. The sweating ceased. Soon I fell asleep.

The next morning was great. My first waking sensation was a stab of pain. I welcomed it. The dread was gone. My body was relaxed. I worked my way out of bed alone, amazed and pleased to discover that a body at peace can take a lot of pain.

I went home the fifth day and was told that the pain would gradually diminish over a period of two weeks. The presence of a wife who was there twenty-four hours a day was a great treasure. Savoring the smells of my wife's cooking was delightful, and eating that delicious food was pleasurable as I looked out at the ocean view. Her presence by my side in the hospital and at home was satisfying beyond description. The sympathy and love shown by Betty, Leroy, Lois, Bob, and Jayne are treasures one cannot buy. Phone calls from all over the country and a stack of cards six inches high were a delight. A warm, friendly, compassionate surgeon, a nurse (actually a very nice person), and aides made up a presence to be appreciated beyond words. What more could one ask for? Yet, none of these wonderful privileges were a substitute for God's comforting presence in my heart.

How does God fill your body with comfort and peace and joy in the presence of pain? I don't know how He does it. But Jesus proved to me that His own words are true: "Come to Me, all you who labor and are heavy laden, and I will give you rest" (Matt. 11:28, NKJV).

He was there all the time, but for two days I depended solely on my bed, water, pills, the presence of skilled medical personnel, and visits by my wife and friends.

You would think that Jesus would say, "You turned your back on Me; now I'll turn my back on you. It's only fair. Call on Me in a few more days after I've nursed My hurt feelings for a while."

No, He kept His word. He was there when I called.

Why did I have to go through the pain of an operation? Why do we even have pain in the world? I don't have all the answers to that question. I just know that when we have circumstances that are difficult, God has provided a way to have peace in the middle of pain.

Two weeks after I came home from the hospital, my wife had a sudden, strange attack. She crawled into bed and stayed there a full day. Our friend Betty came down from her apartment to help. My wife said to us, "Go out of the room and leave me alone. Your presence bothers me." Betty and I just looked at each other. I hobbled out of the room wondering what to do; this wasn't the predictably pleasant Eva that we knew. Something had to be drastically wrong. We called in our doctor neighbor, and he confirmed that something was seriously wrong.

Two days later, after Eva had been to a hospital for some tests, our beloved surgeon called on us in our home: "I'll level with you," he said gravely. "You have an abdominal tumor, Eva. Very likely it is malignant. We must operate at once."

Respond to this statement: "It is just as easy for God to give peace in a minor detail as it is in a difficult circumstance." _____

_____

Examine the Scriptures and/or your answers in today's lesson. Determine the most meaningful thought for you today. Write your thought for the day here:

_____

_____

_____

_____

Applying what God is pointing out to you is essential. How will you apply this truth to your life today? _____

_____

_____

Write a short prayer to God that summarizes your thoughts. _____

_____

_____

_____

_____

Did God bring to mind someone who needs to hear this truth? Who? _____

_____

Thought for the Day:

Physical pain can completely consume your thinking.

◆

DAY FIVE

The Fundamentals of Faith

He left. We sat silently, stunned. Cancer! How can this be? Except for babies, Eva had never been sick. Neither one of us said it, but we both knew we could be staring a painful death in the face. Now, my new hospital experience with Jesus served us well.

Death? Eva?

We decided to review the fundamentals of our faith before the operation. There was no need for her to make the mistake of ignoring God's help as I did.

Fundamental #1: The Other Side of Death is Heaven.

Jesus said: "I go to prepare a place for you. And if I go and prepare a place
for you, I will come again and receive you to Myself; that where I am,
there you may be also."

JOHN 14:2–3, NKJV

For the Christian, the other side of death is heaven. It is a good idea to drop that thought into your mind before stressful conditions swirl around you. I only advise this process for the Christian, however; for the non-Christian, thinking about the other side of death will possibly increase stressful feelings.

Fundamental #2: God Will Provide As Much Strength As You Need In A Day.

God instructed His people: "This day is sacred to our Lord. Do not grieve,
for the joy of the LORD is your strength."

NEHEMIAH 8:10, NIV

This was a precious promise given to the Israelites as Nehemiah repaired the wall and gates around Jerusalem. The project was completed in spite of continuous harassment from Israel's enemies and resistance and criticism from many of his own people. We rested our meager faith on this promise. There would be as much strength as needed in a day, enough to joyfully endure the daily demand.

Fundamental #3: God Provides The Greatest Comfort Available.

[God will comfort] us in all our tribulation, that we may be able to comfort them which are in any trouble, by the comfort wherewith we ourselves are comforted of God. For as the sufferings of Christ abound in us, so our consolation also aboundeth by Christ.

2 Corinthians 1:4–5, kjv

We needed to look to God for comfort, which is not the same as the reassurance that comes from being surrounded by skilled professionals, loving family and friends, good equipment, and medicine. We deeply appreciated human help, but humans could not do what only God could do.

Take a moment to recall a crisis that you, a family member, or a friend endured. Did God help you or them in a way that you could not explain in human terms? Write down your memories of how God gave strength during that difficult time. _____

_____

Did you also have a time of failure when you looked to the world instead of God for comfort? _____

As we prepared to take my wife to the hospital, she decided not to trust her memory. She wrote these verses on three-by-five cards and took them with her:

As thy days, so shall thy strength be.
Deuteronomy 33:25, kjv

For as the sufferings of Christ abound in us, so our consolation also aboundeth by Christ.
2 Corinthians 1:5, kjv

That I may know Him, and the power of His resurrection, and the fellowship of His sufferings.
Philippians 3:10, nkjv

"This day is sacred to our Lord. Do not grieve, for the joy of the Lord is your strength."
Nehemiah 8:10, niv

Let the peace of God rule in your hearts, . . . and be thankful.

COLOSSIANS 3:15, NKJV

These scripture thoughts are extremely helpful during times of crisis. Begin memorizing these when there is no crisis so you will be prepared when the crisis comes.

The operation was over. She had a tube in her nose and down into her stomach. Another tube was attached to the abdominal area. Another one led to a bottle suspended above her head and off to one side. Her operation made mine look like no operation! Yet she seemed to be enveloped in a cocoon of peace. The doctors, nurses, her roommate, and her visitors all noticed it and marveled. Her successful recovery was a serene, peaceful scene in the presence of excruciating pain.

What a contrast to my miserable, unhappy, complaining, self-centered response to the first two days after a minor operation. If you prefer my kind of response, God will honor your choice. On the other hand, He will give you peace and joy *if* you let Him.

How does God do it? He doesn't explain. But by a step of faith, Eva found that she could have peace and joy in her heart when her body was afflicted with seemingly unbearable pain.

When I was a young engineer and struggling to understand what the Christian life was all about, I fell in love with this Bible verse:

"I know whom I have believed and am persuaded that He is able to keep what I have committed to Him until that Day."

2 TIMOTHY 1:12, NKJV

Thirty-five years later, in my wife's hospital room, we knew that you could trust biblical principles. In this crisis, we were not two desperate people thumbing through an unfamiliar book to learn about a strange God. Rather, we were two people reviewing Bible verses and reaching out to a familiar Friend we have tried to follow for thirty-five years.

Billy Graham said it very well:

Mt. Everest was never climbed in a day. Those who attempt to climb its treacherous slopes spend months, even years, in training and practice. Each small mountain conquered prepares one for a higher mountain and a tough climb ahead.

So, too, the best preparation for tough times are the little difficulties and how we react to them . . . You and I are called upon to learn what it means to trust God in every circumstance, and to live for Him no matter what comes our way.

We must think more clearly about suffering and rearrange our priorities so that when Armageddon comes, we will not be taken by surprise or be unprepared. Like Joseph storing up grain for the years of famine that lay ahead, may we store up the truths of God's Word in our hearts as much as possible, so we are prepared for whatever suffering we are called upon to endure.

As an army officer once said, "Weather in war is always favorable if you know how to use it."[2]

Many of us find life hard and full of pain. We cannot avoid these things; but we should not allow our harsh experiences to deaden our sensibilities and to make us stoical or sour. The true problem of living is to keep our hearts sweet and gentle in the hardest conditions and experience.[3]

I am sure that the loving Lord scheduled my operation just before my wife's so that I could appreciate and understand the pain that she experienced.

I also learned that my natural tendency in an unfamiliar traumatic situation was to look for peace after the end of the difficult circumstances, rather than obtain peace from God in the middle of the circumstances. When my wife and I focused on the Lord before and after her surgery, we both found that there was a world of difference in the peace in our hearts.

Based on my own personal experience, I recommend that everyone seek God *before* any operation or crisis. Take time alone or together and write down the Bible verses that you feel apply to your situation. Don't make my mistake! Quickly invite the Lord into every crisis.

Examine the Scriptures and/or your answers in today's lesson. Determine the most meaningful thought for you today. Write your thought for the day here:

_____

_____

_____

Applying what God is pointing out to you is essential. How will you apply this truth to your life today? _____

_____

Write a short prayer to God that summarizes your thoughts._____

_____

_____

_____

Did God bring to mind someone who needs to hear this truth? Who?_____

_____

Thought for the Day:

The time to prepare for a crisis is when there is no crisis.

◆

(Optional—But Recommended!)

Bring forward your thoughts from each day:

1. _____
2. _____
3. _____
4. _____
5. _____

Bring forward your application:

1. _____
2. _____
3. _____
4. _____
5. _____

Bring forward your prayers:

1. _____
2. _____
3. _____
4. _____
5. _____

Bring forward who you shared your thoughts with:

1. _____
2. _____
3. _____
4. _____
5. _____

Thought for the Week:

Any crisis is a trigger to focus on God.

◆

Anger Is One Letter Away
from Danger

Thought Starter:

Is being a little bit angry like being a little bit pregnant?

◆

Memory Verse for the Week:

But now you must also put off all these: anger, wrath, malice . . .
Colossians 3:8, nkjv

DAY ONE

Facing Anger Honestly

It is not very often that an author describes a session with his counselor. Jay Carty did just that and I happened to be the counselor.

I was on my way to teach a class at a Christian college when I was given a note requesting that I return a long distance phone call from Jay. I returned his call and he wanted to set up an appointment. We agreed on 2:00 P.M. that day and I hurried on to teach my class. In my rush to get to class on time, I did not make any notation about the appointment.

After class, a student invited me to play racquetball at 1:30 P.M. Our play was interrupted by a phone call: Jay Carty wanted to know why I hadn't kept my appointment.

I showered and dressed as quickly as possible, but I was still about an hour late. On the way to the appointment I breathed a prayer to the Lord to help me handle a very embarrassing situation. I walked into the room where a very understandably irate Jay Carty, six feet, seven inches tall, former professional basketball player and all muscle, was waiting with his wife. To say the least, there was a very awkward beginning. I mumbled an apology and tried to explain that I took the call on my way to a class and failed to write the time in my schedule.

Jay handed me a folder containing his Taylor/Johnson Temperament Test. I could feel him glaring at me as I studied it and realized that he could be very intimidating to most people when he was angry. The test showed an extremely dominant, very hostile, strongly expressive person. I decided to take a highly aggressive approach. After all, he must have some biblical insights since he had been a camp director in a Christian camp and was now considering moving on to serve in another Christian organization.

Here is Jay's version of the meeting:

I had been directing a Christian conference center in the mountains of southern California around Lake Arrowhead. The big problems at the camp had been solved, and I knew I wasn't a fine tuner organizationally. The camp needed a true manager for the next step in its history.

I had two job options, but I couldn't decide between them. I was either going with "Churches Alive," a discipleship organization, as their Northwest Director, or I was going to be the Team Director for Athletes in Action basketball, a ministry of Campus Crusade for Christ.

I kept vacillating. My kids were saying, "What kind of a day is it, Dad, a Churches Alive day or an A. I. A. day?" Sometimes my indecision varied hourly.

I just couldn't make up my mind; it was really tough. So we went to see Dr. Henry Brandt, a nationally acclaimed Christian counselor, and now teaching at a Christian college. I needed help, and I hoped he could give it.

San Diego is a three-hour drive from Lake Arrowhead. When Mary and I arrived, Dr. Brandt wasn't there. He had forgotten the meeting and showed up a half hour late. I was a bit upset about waiting after such a long drive.

We took our Taylor/Johnson Temperament Analysis Tests with us. When we went into the office, the good doctor spread out the tests, looked at them, and asked, "What's the problem?"

I said, "I'm having trouble making a job change and thought you could help us sort out the decision-making process."

"Well, it's easy for me to see what the problem is, Jay," Henry responded. "There's sin in your life."

After a lengthy pause I offered a rather impatient response, "Henry, perhaps you could elaborate just a little bit."

Dr. Brandt spent the next three or four minutes undressing me emotionally. I was sitting there naked in front of him; he could see who I really was, and I knew it. I was upset. Now, you probably wouldn't have known I was mad. My wife knew. Henry knew, because he's a pro.

So, I'm sitting there mad, and Henry asks, "What seems to be bothering you, Jay?"

"Nothing!"

"Don't compound the problem by lying about it; tell me what's on your mind."

Well, he picked the right guy. My Taylor/ Johnson scored me 99 percent dominant, 96 percent hostile, strongly expressive, and placed me considerably more subjective than objective. In other words, I'm a walking time bomb. Apart from the Holy Spirit, I'm dangerous.

"You hotshot." I was indignant. "You don't care about me, or you wouldn't have forgotten the appointment. Then you pull this grandstand move by telling me there's sin in my life, pat me on the rear, send me on my way and tell me, 'Hey, you just talked to the great Dr. Henry Brandt.' Well, thank you, but I'm not impressed. I think you're a fraud, and I think you stink."

He disarmed me with a totally emotionless question, "What else seems to be bothering you, Jay?"

There wasn't much fight left in me by this time. It's so hard to fight with someone who won't fight. I said, "Henry, never mind. Just forget abut the whole thing." I motioned to Mary for us to leave.

Henry said, "No, no, don't go. Right now, how do you feel down in the pit of your stomach? Would you say the fruit of the Spirit, as defined in Galatians 5:22 and 23, typifies the way you feel: "love, joy, peace, patience, kindness, goodness, faithfulness, gentleness, and self-control?"

"That answer's easy," I snorted. "None of those qualities typify the way I feel, at least not right now."

He asked, "Then it's safe to conclude you are not filled with the Spirit of God?"

What are the characteristics of a person *not controlled* by the Spirit of God? _

_____

_____

_____

Is it easy for you to know when a friend, family member, or your own self is *not controlled* by the Spirit of God?_____

That question means lots of different things to lots of different people. Some people are really asking if you speak in tongues, but that wasn't what Henry was asking. Some people would be asking if you truly know Jesus as Savior. That wasn't what Henry was asking either. He wanted to know if I was currently experiencing the power of God in my life.

I put on my sarcastically theological facade and replied, "Now, Henry, I know Jesus Christ as Savior. My body is the dwelling place of the Holy Spirit. The Holy Spirit's in there. I've been sealed with the Holy Spirit of promise, I've been baptized into one body, and I drink of the same Spirit you do. But if what you're talking about is the essence of Ephesians 5:18 (being constantly in the process of being filled or empowered by the Holy Spirit), then I'm not filled. Oh, it's true, the Spirit's in here," as I pointed to my body, "but right now he doesn't have all of me. I'm mad, and I've spent some time dwelling on my anger. As I understand it, until he has 100 percent of me, I'm not filled. If that's what you're talking about, then I'm not filled because none of the qualities you just mentioned are currently evident in my life."

"That's right," he said. "If the qualities aren't there, you can't be filled." He asked again, "You're sure you're not filled?"

"I'm sure," I growled. "Right now I'm not filled, I'm real mad. I mean, I'm really mad at you, and I'm not handling it well. Henry, you may not know it, but your upper lip is in danger of being pulled up over your forehead."

Remember, I ran a Christian camp, and in Christian camping you live on the grounds, and everybody with whom you work lives on the grounds. In other words, you live with the same people you work with. You can't get away from each other, except by going into your living quarters. So when you get one or two fellow workers who irritate you, you're irritated most of the time. That was me for sure.

It was then he asked me the blockbuster question. He asked gently, in a soft voice that was such a contrast to mine, "Jay, do you feel that way most of the time?"

It was so quiet you could hear our breathing.

"Yes."

*Is it easier for you to see anger in someone else, or to admit your own anger? Why?*_____

_____

_____

It was true. Anger was an ongoing problem for me. I guess it started early in my life. Anger is often a problem for people who have had an alcoholic parent and who went through their parent's divorce during early teenage years. I had quit a good job, an executive position. We sold a wonderful home in Corona del Mar in the Newport Beach area of southern California, with a view of the sun setting behind Catalina Island every night. We had keys to a private beach. I worked four minutes from my house and actually went home for lunch each day. Talk about having it made! We did, but we flicked it all in to go serve God. Then, four-and-a-half years later, I discovered I'd been serving Him in the power of my flesh, not in the power of the Spirit. You see, I was mad most of the time.

I said, "Henry, how bad am I? What am I going to do? I've only spent a lifetime learning to live this way."

"It's like having a splinter in your thumb," Henry responded. "You hurt your thumb a lot because you use it a lot. But if you pull the splinter, the thumb gets well rather quickly."

"Please tell me how."

"Confess it to God. "

I was still puzzled. "What are you talking about? How?" I was pleading now.

"Whenever you feel anger, talk to God about it before you sin. You might have to do it twenty times the first day, but it will only require eighteen the second. As you practice, your confession frequency will continue to decrease. You might go a few days or even a week or so without having to do it.[1]

Is there a problem in your life that you have to deal with day after day? Do you want to get rid of the problem? What did you learn in this story that applies to your problem? _____

_____

Jay Carty was a man who had wrestled most of his life with anger. He experienced a miracle with his anger. I didn't solve his anger problem; God did. Today, he is an easygoing, cheerful, gentle person. What made the difference? He got hold of the simple truth that Jesus died to save us from our sins and make His Spirit available to us. He trained himself to be alert to the first signs of anger, turn at once to God for cleansing, and to be empowered by God's Holy Spirit. Today, Jay has an ever-widening speaking ministry in which he teaches people how to yield themselves to God's control.

During my meeting with Jay and his wife, I did not go into his past feelings toward his father or his mother or how his parents' divorce affected him when he was younger. Our discussion lasted twenty to thirty minutes and focused on his sinful behavior of anger. I just directed him to the healing power of God in order to deal with the sin in his life today. God may have later brought issues from his past to his mind that needed attention, but the immediate issue was his current anger. This is the miracle available to everyone: we are a prayer away from peace and freedom from anger.

Do you believe you are just a prayer away from peace and freedom from anger? Why do you believe that you are or are not? _____

_____

How fast can someone become angry? Five seconds is not too fast, is it? If I can get angry in less than five seconds, I can get un-angry in the time it takes to breathe a simple prayer. It *is* just that simple! It has worked in my own life and in thousands of lives over the years.

It *is* also true that I don't understand the complete situation in people's lives. And neither do you or any other counselor! But God does! That's why we bring our anger to Him: He understands us and loves us and wants us to be free from anger.

Examine the Scriptures and/or your answers in today's lesson. Determine the most meaningful thought for you today. Write your thought for the day here:

_____

_____

_____

Applying what God is pointing out to you is essential. How will you apply this truth to your life today? _____

_____

_____

Write a short prayer to God that summarizes your thoughts._____

_____

_____

_____

Did God bring to mind someone who needs to hear this truth? Who?_____

_____

Thought for the Day:
You are just a prayer away from peace and freedom from anger.

◆

DAY TWO

The Consuming Nature of Anger

Some people relish and enjoy their anger. Frederick Bueckner says it clearly:

> Of the Seven Deadly Sins, anger is possibly the most fun. To lick your wounds, to smack your lips over grievances long past, to roll over your tongue the prospect of bitter confrontations still to come, to savor to the last toothsome morsel both the pain you are given and the pain you are giving back; in many ways it is a feast fit for a king. The chief drawback is that what you are wolfing down is yourself. *The skeleton at the feast is you.*"[2]

I have never met anyone, anywhere in the world, who has escaped the destructive force of anger, or who has never experienced someone else's anger as a destructive force. The one single problem that everyone is plagued with universally, is anger.

Some writers say anger is neither good nor bad. It all depends on how you use it. Some writers use the term "righteous indignation" which motivates a person to correct mistreatment and injustices; if this is correct, then people will be angry the rest of their lives because there is always something you can be angry about. Some go so far as to say that anger is God-given.

The Latin root for anger is *angere* which means "to strangle." I find that the definition of anger helps clarify the real situation:

ANGER: emotional reaction, of displeasure and/or antagonism; an impulse to retaliate, punish, seek revenge. Anger can vary in intensity from mild annoyance that is hardly noticeable to extreme overmastering rage resembling insanity. Anger can trigger an outward display ranging from a light change of expression to destruction or murder; from a mild word to enraged screaming.

Personally, I have never experienced anger within my body as a positive force. It has *always* been a hindrance to intelligent straight thinking and constructive rational behavior. And in my work as a counselor and business consultant, I have never observed anger to be a positive factor in problem solving. I have never found anger to be righteous. From the slightest shade of anger that we may not even be conscious of to the anger that leads to murder, it is all cut from the same cloth.

In an instant, anger can change a person from being satisfied, cheerful, and relaxed to being dissatisfied, unhappy, and tense. Oddly enough, this sudden change within the body is triggered by something that happens outside the body. Life would be much more pleasant and comfortable and relaxing if only we could find its cause and cure.

How would you describe your characteristics when you are angry?_____

_____

_____

_____

How would or do others describe you when you are angry? _____

_____

_____

Do you usually know when a close friend or family member is angry? _____

_____

How do you know?_____

_____

_____

If there is a topic about which there is universal agreement, it would be that unrestrained anger can destroy us. It cannot be ignored. It must be tamed.

But if there is a topic about which there is universal disagreement, it would be how to tame anger.

If there is anger in your heart, someone may either do or not do something that instantly triggers anger inside of you. Someone may say or not say something that immediately triggers your anger. Something happens or fails to happen that triggers your anger. Thoughts about the past, present, or future can trigger your anger. Angry emotions can vary in intensity from mild annoyance that is hardly noticeable to extreme overmastering rage that resembles insanity.

Examine the Scriptures and/or your answers in today's lesson. Determine the most meaningful thought for you today. Write your thought for the day here:

_____

_____

_____

_____

Applying what God is pointing out to you is essential. How will you apply this truth to your life today? _____

_____

_____

Write a short prayer to God that summarizes your thoughts._____

_____

_____

_____

_____

Did God bring to mind someone who needs to hear this truth? Who?_____

_____

Thought for the Day:

Unrestrained anger can destroy you. It cannot be ignored. It must be tamed.

◆

DAY THREE

The Physical Aspects of Anger

Anger produces disagreeable bodily changes that cannot be ignored. Almost everyone is familiar with the following:

- ◆ pulse rate increases
- ◆ heart beats faster
- ◆ blood pressure rises
- ◆ the throat tightens
- ◆ mouth is dry
- ◆ gooseflesh appears
- ◆ hair is erect
- ◆ pupils of the eyes open wide
- ◆ eyeballs glisten
- ◆ person sweats, blushes, turns pale
- ◆ muscles tense
- ◆ highly alert
- ◆ desire for physical action increases
- ◆ insomnia may be present
- ◆ problems with the colon and/or stomach problems appear

Anger can trigger some action ranging from just a slight change of expression to destruction or murder. Anger may result in a mild word or enraged screaming. Anger can, but seldom does, motivate a person to seek changes that will improve the environment that triggers the anger.

How do people tend to respond when they are around noticeably angry people?

_____

_____

To grasp how frustrating anger can be, look at the range of people who can trigger an anger response in you: babies, parents, marriage partners, children, friends, people at work, total strangers, yourself, clerks, neighbors, officials, people in social gatherings.

Circumstances can also trigger anger. The range varies greatly. P. T. Young reports the results of asking a group of college students to keep records of what stimulated them to an angry reaction. Here are the results: unjust accusations, insulting remarks, not invited to a party, disobedience of children, criticisms, contradictions, scoldings, unwelcome advice, work left undone, being locked out, money being lost, sleep interrupted, physical pain, thwarting self-expression.[3]

Recently, someone even told me that he was angry at the weather. I am sure that you can also add to the above list.

The question is: "Can God help?" The answer is emphatically, "Yes!" His help is decidedly different from human or self-help.

Examine the Scriptures and/or your answers in today's lesson. Determine the most meaningful thought for you today. Write your thought for the day here:

_____

_____

_____

_____

Applying what God is pointing out to you is essential. How will you apply this truth to your life today? _____

_____

Write a short prayer to God that summarizes your thoughts. _____

_____

_____

_____

Did God bring to mind someone who needs to hear this truth? Who?_____

_____

Thought for the Day:
Bottled up anger can ruin your health.

♦

D A Y   F O U R

The Biblical View
of Anger

Many people who know very little about Jesus do know that He threw the moneychangers out of the temple.

Search the following Scripture passages: Matthew 21:12–15; Mark 11:15–18; and Luke 19:45–47. After reading these passages, did you discover any Scriptures that said Jesus was angry when He drove the moneychangers out of the temple? Also, what was Jesus doing immediately after he drove the moneychangers out of the temple?_____

_____

Others who know very little about the Bible know about another verse: "Be ye angry, and sin not: let not the sun go down upon your wrath" (Eph. 4:26, KJV).

How would you explain this verse to another person?_____

_____

People use these few verses to justify their anger. I take this verse to mean that if you are aware of being angry you should deal with it quickly. The deadline is sundown.

Anger is a normal response to unrighteousness. Are we to conclude, then, that our anger is God-given and alerts and energizes us into action to see that wrongs are made right?

Assuming that there are people or issues worthy of focusing wrath upon, what or who would they be? _____

_____

_____

As I study the Bible, I do not find that we are instructed to vent our anger against evil causes or toward evil people. Evaluate these verses:

"Love your enemies, bless those who curse you, do good to those who hate you, and pray for those who spitefully use you and persecute you . . . [The Father] makes His sun rise on the evil and on the good."
MATTHEW 5:44–45, NKJV

Husbands, love your wives, just as Christ also loved the church and gave Himself for it.
EPHESIANS 5:25, NKJV

Teach the young women to be sober, to love their husbands, to love their children.
TITUS 2:4, KJV

"You shall love your neighbor as yourself."
MATTHEW 22:39, NKJV

Dear friends, never avenge yourselves. Leave that to God, for he has said that he will repay those who deserve it.
ROMANS 12:19, TLB

Love the brotherhood.
1 PETER 2:17, NKJV

Abound in love . . . for all men.
1 THESSALONIANS 3:12, NASB

If we eliminate all of the above people as objects of our anger, who is scripturally left that can be the object of our anger?

The Bible does state that anger is a natural expression of our humanness; it is a natural expression of our "old man" and "the old sin nature." But the Bible says that anger is "sin" and it is not okay.

Look at what the Bible actually says about man's anger:

The wrath of man does not produce the righteousness of God.
JAMES 1:20, NKJV

Cease from anger, and forsake wrath; do not fret—it only causes harm.
PSALM 37:8, NKJV

Do not hasten in your spirit to be angry, For anger rests in the bosom of fools.
ECCLESIASTES 7:9, NKJV

Make no friendship with an angry man, and with a furious man do not go, lest you learn his ways and set a snare for your soul.
PROVERBS 22:24–25, NKJV

A quick-tempered man acts foolishly.
PROVERBS 14:17, NASB

He who is slow to anger is better than the mighty, and he who rules his spirit than he who takes a city.
PROVERBS 16:32, NKJV

"Whoever is angry with his brother without a cause shall be in danger of the judgment."
MATTHEW 5:22, NKJV

Let all bitterness, wrath, anger, clamor, and evil speaking be put away from you, with all malice.
EPHESIANS 4:31, NKJV

Put off all these: anger, wrath, malice.
COLOSSIANS 3:8, NKJV

[Lay] aside all malice.
1 PETER 2:1, NKJV

What conclusion do you have about anger after reading these Bible passages?

_____

_____

Anger is a universal fact of life. Law enforcement people report that at least half of the homicides committed in this country involve people who know each other. Millions of women are beaten up each year by their husbands. Millions of children are abused each year by angry parents. At any time it seems that people experience an explosion of varying degrees of intensity of displeasure, antagonism, belligerence, rage, and violent passion.

The difficult problem is how can a human being who naturally responds angrily to the circumstances of life change from responding in anger to responding in love? Humanly speaking, we must admit that this biblical advice is impossible to attain. We all know that to bottle up or swallow your anger is no solution. Bottled-up anger can ruin your health, twist your thinking, and make you a walking time bomb, set to explode at some external provocation. What can a person do? You can attempt to manage this anger yourself or you can turn to God for help. Humanly speaking, what can you do to tame your anger?

What advice would you give to someone who wanted a human way to tame their anger? _____

_____

_____

_____

Children are a large group that are victims of anger expression. Some advice was proposed in a newspaper advertisement by the National Committee for Prevention of Child Abuse. It was entitled *12 Alternatives to Whacking Your Kid.* The ad advised that when big and little problems of your everyday life pile up to the point where you feel like lashing out, stop! Take time out. Don't take it out on your kid. Try any or all of these simple alternatives—whatever works for you. The ad goes on to list twelve:

1. Stop in your tracks. Step back. Sit down.
2. Take five deep breaths. Inhale. Exhale, slowly, slowly.
3. Count to ten. Better yet, twenty. Or say the alphabet out loud.
4. Phone a friend. A relative. Even the weather.
5. Still mad? Punch a pillow. Or munch an apple.
6. Thumb through a magazine, book, newspaper, photo album.
7. Do some sit-ups.
8. Pick up a pencil and write down your thoughts.
9. Take a hot bath, or a cold shower.
10. Lie down on the floor, or just put your feet up.
11. Put on your favorite record.
12. Water your plants.

I was reading an article on anger management while traveling in an airplane. This is typical advice offered by anger management professionals. The authors proposed four steps:

1. *Cool off before you sound off.* They made suggestions similar to the newspaper ad.

2. *Identify what causes you to feel anger.* How do you take criticism or teasing? Develop an awareness of what triggers your anger.

3. *How can you make anger work for you?* Learn what forms of anger expression are acceptable to your colleagues. Find something constructive that you can do to work off your anger.

4. *Communicate your anger.* Use facts and objective information that others need to know about you. Help them see that your response was appropriate and reasonable. Develop information so you can help each other avoid anger-producing situations.[4]

Is it really true that we must live with angry responses all our lives? Is there no other way to find freedom from anger than in perfecting self-control, resolving human-relation problems, and altering the circumstances we get plunged into? Is there no other way than to back off and calm down?

As far as I know, that's all anyone humanly speaking knows to do at this point in history. This is the struggle that the humanist must live with because anger happens so fast you often act before you know it.

The Bible offers a radical solution: "Put it away. Stop it." This is humanly impossible. Yes, it takes a miracle. You need supernatural help.

Examine the Scriptures and/or your answers in today's lesson. Determine the most meaningful thought for you today. Write your thought for the day here:

_____

_____

_____

Applying what God is pointing out to you is essential. How will you apply this truth to your life today? _____

_____

_____

Write a short prayer to God that summarizes your thoughts. _____

_____

_____

_____

Did God bring to mind someone who needs to hear this truth? Who?_____

_____

Thought for the Day:
Reading the Bible will help you understand that anger is sin.

◆

DAY FIVE

Dealing with Anger Biblically

There are two basic steps in dealing with anger from a biblical perspective.

1. Recognize anger as sin.

God's prescription for dealing with destructive anger is precise and strong. Strife, malice, hatred, anger, outbursts of wrath, dissension, and contention are works of the flesh which are of the sinful nature (Gal. 5:19–21).

Anger is sin, and that's good news! Because, there is a divine solution for sin. God promised to help you. Dealing with sin is His specialty.

> [Jesus] will save His people from their sins.
> MATTHEW 1:21, NKJV

> Nor is there salvation in any other, for there is no other name under heaven given among men by which we must be saved.
> ACTS 4:12, NKJV

A simple step that gives you the strength to "stop" angry responses is to invite Jesus to come into your life. Competent, able people have a hard time accepting the fact that we need supernatural help. "I can manage my anger. Isn't that good enough?" It certainly beats exploding. The best you can do is to manage your anger. Only God can help you to "stop" because *anger is sin.* Therefore, humans need a Savior who will cleanse us of our sins.

It is not inevitable that we must spend the rest of our lives struggling with anger. Anger can be "put away." Once we accept the fact that anger is sin and we need a Savior, we can practice a simple biblical directive daily, if necessary: "If we confess our sins, He is faithful and just to forgive us our sins and to cleanse us from all unrighteousness" (1 John 1:9, NKJV).

What do you think God meant when He shared 1 John 1:9 with you? Check your responses.

❏ God will cleanse us from all our unrighteousness.

❏ God can forgive us our sins but it doesn't solve our problems.

❏ Jesus is sufficient to cleanse us from all our sin, even anger.

❏ Jesus died so we could be free from our sin.

He will cleanse the anger out of our hearts. Anger is not good. Anger interferes with my thinking process. It is bad. It is destructive. It is sin.

2. Replace anger with the fruit of the Spirit.

When you have a forgiven, cleansed heart, you can ask God for the power of the Holy Spirit to produce the fruit of the Spirit in your life: "Love, joy, peace, longsuffering, kindness, goodness, faithfulness, gentleness, self-control" (Gal. 5:22–23, NKJV).

You will still have problems, face injustices and difficult people just as everyone does. You will still need to be energized, alerted, and motivated to correct what needs correcting. But God knows that a person energized by the Holy Spirit with love, joy, peace, longsuffering, kindness, goodness, faithfulness, gentleness, and self-control has the strength to conquer bitterness, sarcastic words, anxiety, bodily tensions, or violent behavior that formerly characterized him.

The apostle Paul says it best: "Walk in the Spirit, and you shall not fulfill the lust of the flesh" (Gal. 5:16, NKJV).

A Christian does not always surrender to God perfectly, anymore than he can manage himself perfectly. Few people make it through any given day perfectly. But you can catch anger at the earliest possible point. When you realize you have sinned, take it to God.

As the apostle John says: "My little children, these things I write to you, that you may not sin. And if anyone sins, we have an Advocate with the Father, Jesus Christ the righteous. And He Himself is the propitiation [the one who paid our debt with his life] for our sins, and not for ours only but also for the whole world" (1 John 2:1–2, NKJV).

Examine the Scriptures and/or your answers in today's lesson. Determine the most meaningful thought for you today. Write your thought for the day here:

_____

_____

_____

_____

Applying what God is pointing out to you is essential. How will you apply this truth to your life today? _____

_____

_____

Write a short prayer to God that summarizes your thoughts._____

_____

_____

_____

_____

Did God bring to mind someone who needs to hear this truth? Who?_____

_____

Thought for the Day:

Anger must be removed and the fruit of the Spirit must be
the replacement.

♦

(Optional—But Recommended!)

Bring forward your thoughts from each day:

1. _____

2. _____

3. _____

4. _____

5. _____

Bring forward your application:

1. _____
2. _____
3. _____
4. _____
5. _____

Bring forward your prayers:

1. _____
2. _____
3. _____
4. _____
5. _____

Bring forward who you shared your thoughts with:

1. _____
2. _____
3. _____
4. _____
5. _____

Thought for the Week:

Anger puts my brain on the shelf; God's supernatural miracle
puts my anger on the shelf.

◆

UNIT TEN

Your Wife Has Inoperable Cancer

Thought Starter:

Is the peace of God that guards your heart and mind available
in a crisis?

◆

Memory Verse for the Week:

**Be anxious for nothing, but in everything by prayer and supplication, with
thanksgiving, let your requests be made known to God; and the peace of
God, which surpasses all understanding, will guard your hearts and
minds through Christ Jesus.**

PHILIPPIANS 4:6–7, NKJV

DAY ONE

God's Peace Is Beyond Our Human Understanding

It had been about two years since Eva had her operation. Her cancer problem was behind her, and we had planned to spend Thanksgiving with our daughter, Beth, and her family. Instead, Eva was in a hospital in Florida. Shortly after Eva had been wheeled into the operating room, the surgeon came to us with the chilling and terrifying news that she had inoperable cancer and had six months to a year to live.

At first, the news left us stunned! Surely, we thought, there must be a way to overcome this problem. The doctors proposed a combination of chemical and radiation therapy. Eva and I didn't sleep well for several nights as we absorbed the reality of this news.

We were forced to take an in-depth look at just what peace is. We had spent the previous thirty-five years studying and searching for correct principles to live by. Most of what we had found was from the Bible, and we had traveled the world trying to teach what we had learned. Over the years, the most common problem we had seen was people who were struggling in their quest for peace. Now, we were being given one of life's acid tests: can you have peace during a painful death?

Together we found several verses that directed us to the God of peace:

Now may the Lord of peace Himself give you peace always in every way.
The Lord be with you all.
2 Thessalonians 3:16, NKJV

Be anxious for nothing, but in everything by prayer and supplication, with thanksgiving, let your requests be made known to God; and the peace of God, which surpasses all understanding, will guard your hearts and minds through Christ Jesus.

PHILIPPIANS 4:6–7, NKJV

"These things I have spoken to you, that in Me you may have peace. In the world you will have tribulation; but be of good cheer, I have overcome the world."

JOHN 16:33, NKJV

Let the peace of God rule in your heart, . . . and be thankful.

COLOSSIANS 3:15, NKJV

These verses made it clear that peace is something that originates with God and is available to us under any conditions, which included our present circumstances. Philippians 4:6–7 indicated clearly that God's peace is beyond our human understanding. Even though it is real and I have experienced it over the years, I still don't understand it and can't really explain it. It just works.

Picture a peaceful person with relaxed muscles, normal blood pressure, a quiet mind, and a calm and contented heart. Consider the opposite: tense, anxious, stressful, and uneasy. We had to face the fact that we were not peaceful.

Take a moment to examine your present physical condition. Be honest. Would you say that at the present moment your mind and body are:
- ❏ Relaxed
- ❏ Tense
- ❏ Worried
- ❏ Contented

How can you be peaceful when you face a painful, slow death? How can you be peaceful when you have tough decisions to make? For example, what do you do about a specialist's recommendation that you undergo chemical and radiation therapy and when another specialist doesn't recommend it? When you pray and ask God for guidance and there is only silence? When you receive solicited and unsolicited conflicting advice from many friends and associates who care deeply?

Think about a particular crisis in your life in which you received different kinds of advice. How did you finally arrive at the solution to your problem?_____

_____

Was the conclusion that you came to the right conclusion?_____

_____

We turned to our Guidebook for help. These were the time-proven instructions that we already knew and they needed to be applied to our new circumstances. Never before had we faced a situation like this one.

"Trust in the LORD with all your heart, and lean not on your own understanding. In all your ways acknowledge Him, and He shall direct your paths" (Prov. 3:5–6, NKJV).

If you combine this verse with Philippians 4:6–7 and John 16:33, it is clear that if you want to get a hearing from God you need to present your "requests" to Him in a relaxed, cheerful, thankful, trusting fashion. We may have an opinion about how things should turn out, but we need to be neutral about how they actually do turn out.

Examine the Scriptures and/or your answers in today's lesson. Determine the most meaningful thought for you today. Write your thought for the day here:

_____

_____

_____

_____

Applying what God is pointing out to you is essential. How will you apply this truth to your life today? _____

_____

_____

Write a short prayer to God that summarizes your thoughts. _____

_____

_____

_____

Did God bring to mind someone who needs to hear this truth? Who? _____

_____

Thought for the Day:

If you want to receive peace from God you need to present your "requests" to Him in a relaxed, cheerful, thankful, trusting fashion.

◆

D A Y   T W O

The Anxiety of a Crisis

Eva and I had very definite opinions about how this situation should turn out. She had always been a healthy woman. We wanted her to be healed! Why should a good woman who has been faithful to God, her husband, and her family suffer a slow painful death by cancer? It didn't make sense. Of course we were anxious! Why shouldn't we be?

Do you agree that we *should* be anxious? Why or why not? _____

_____

_____

But the Bible said we needed to come to the Lord in the proper spirit. The Bible said to relax and trust God. We asked the Lord to help us, and we experienced a miracle. He did calm us down, and we were able to trust Him.

Eva decided that she didn't want the chemical and radiation therapy. Our research indicated that this might prolong her life a bit, but only at the cost of intense suffering. She preferred to try a special diet and food supplement program.

When we let a specialist and some of our friends know about our decision, we experienced a chorus of intensive opposition. I was confronted by some of our best friends who said we must avail ourselves of the finest medical technique available. They insisted I would never be able to forgive myself if I didn't do this.

What advice would you give a friend if they were doing something that they believed was right yet most of their friends were telling them to do something different? _____

_____

_____

When the judgment of people we respected was so strong against our decision, Eva and I had to reconsider. We prayed fervently for direction. Silence.

I remembered a time when Moses was in need of direction. He cried out to the Lord, and the Lord gave him this answer: "My Presence will go with you, and I will give you rest" (Ex. 33:14, NKJV).

That seemed to be our answer. Eva did not change her mind and we proceeded with our plan. We discovered that we could not commit our ways unto Him once and for all. We found ourselves drifting away again and again from peaceful trust in God.

Eva could not follow the rigorous diet and food supplement program that she had selected. Slowly she lost weight: 120 pounds, 110 pounds, 100 pounds, 90 pounds. Sincerely concerned people came to call on us. They asked about our faith. A prayer of faith should heal her. We were asked if there was any known sin in our lives. We appreciated their interest. We searched our hearts and as best we could tell, there was nothing that blocked our prayers for healing.

Several dear people proposed that our faith was too weak. They would pray for Eva themselves, and we could benefit from their faith.

Eva just lost more weight and got weaker and weaker. She stuck to her decision not to have chemical therapy. Weeks grew into months as we observed a steady physical decline. At the same time, our faith and trust in the Lord grew. We realized that peace was not dependent on God doing what we wanted Him to do, but peace was dependent on knowing that He was God, and He knew what was best in every situation.

Our daughter Sue was able to spend the last six months of Eva's life with her. She was a missionary with the North American Indian Mission, which we had worked with since she was a teenager. Now that Eva was sick, the mission assigned her to look after her mother. I canceled most of my itinerary and also spent the last six months of her life with her. Numerous other people spent several days to a week helping to keep the home going. Our whole family gathered together for Christmas. Mel and Bertha Willett spent five or six weeks near the end of Eva's life. Tom and Ruth Tate, dear friends for thirty years, took a week out of a very busy life to be with Eva. We were surrounded by many people from all over the world; they offered sympathy, friendship, and help with housekeeping, cooking, and running errands.

Can you remember a crisis in which God blessed you with friends who helped you endure the crisis? _____

_____

Did they help you deal with the anxiety of the crisis? _____

What did you learn that would help others in their anxiety? _____

_____

_____

Examine the Scriptures and/or your answers in today's lesson. Determine the most meaningful thought for you today. Write your thought for the day here:

_____

_____

_____

_____

Applying what God is pointing out to you is essential. How will you apply this truth to your life today? _____

_____

_____

Write a short prayer to God that summarizes your thoughts. _____

_____

_____

_____

_____

Did God bring to mind someone who needs to hear this truth? Who? _____

_____

Thought for the Day:

Peaceful trust in God will cure anxiety even in the midst of a crisis.

◆

DAY   THREE

Trusting God in
All Circumstances

Notwithstanding the prayers of people all over the world, Eva continued to fail. One day it hit me more clearly than ever that she would die. It made me mad, and I let God know it! Like many people in my situation, I had refused to accept the obvious. One day as I was leaving our condominium, walking toward the elevator and venting my wrath at God, a presence seemed to be in that hallway. It was as if a voice spoke: "Trust me. I am God. Let Me comfort you and give you peace. I will not change Eva's condition. You want to be angry and rebellious about it. I want you to let Me change your heart."

Once more, I needed to return to trusting God. I needed to repent and let Him calm me down again, and again commit Eva into His loving care.

What is the Christian's correct response to anxiety? Check your response:

❏ Try not to think about the crisis.
❏ Talk to a good friend about your anxiety.
❏ Pray to God, repenting of anxiety, and ask God to help you trust Him.
❏ Pray and hope for the thoughts to go away.

About six weeks before she died, Eva told me the pain was becoming more intense. She became so preoccupied with her pain that she couldn't think about anything else. She asked me to keep reminding her to look to God for peace. When she was relaxed, she said, the pain was less.

We prayed for wisdom. About that time, Dr. Steiner from Buffalo dropped in to see us. He taught us some relaxation techniques that helped greatly to relieve her pain. Together, Eva and I asked the Lord to teach us how to help her to be peaceful. We created a plan that combined physical relaxation and yielding her heart to the Lord.

For physical relaxation we did what Dr. Steiner taught us. I would kneel beside the bed and whisper to Eva, "Tighten your toe muscles and let them go. Tighten your foot muscles and let them go. Tighten your ankle muscles and let them go. Tighten your calf muscles and let them go." We worked this way with all the muscles from the bottom of her feet to the top of her head. I will be eternally grateful to Dr. Steiner for his help.

In addition, we chose some Scripture verses that I repeated after the physical relaxation exercises. I would whisper:

This is the day which the Lord has made; We will rejoice and be glad in it.
PSALM 118:24, NKJV

This day is sacred to our Lord. Do not grieve, for the joy of the LORD is your strength.
NEHEMIAH 8:10, NIV

Let the peace of God rule in your hearts, . . . and be thankful.
COLOSSIANS 3:15, NKJV

Then I would whisper, "Let the Lord give you peace. Just let Him give you joy. You need more today than you ever needed in your whole life." By the time we finished this, she had drifted away into blessed, peaceful sleep.

We repeated this routine six, eight, ten times in a day. Sometimes she would call me; sometimes on my own I felt the urge to go to her. We looked forward to these little meetings, and we actually "enjoyed" them in that we both knew we were participants in something beyond human understanding.

Can you think of other Scripture passages that teach Christians to trust God in all circumstances? If not, look in a Bible concordance or topical Bible and search for other passages. Record your findings here: _____

_____

_____

Can you think of any Scriptures that tell you not to trust God? _____

_____

I do not for a moment discount the wonderful support, affection, sympathy, and help given to us by beloved friends. We had the best that human beings can give.

However, we all witnessed something supernatural happening to Eva in those last several weeks of her life.

She continued to lose weight until she was down to seventy pounds. She became more and more serene as the end neared. There was a kind of angelic aura of joyful peace about her.

She allowed the peace of God that surpasses understanding to guard her heart and mind through Jesus Christ. This was Eva's final word by living it out in her life: "[Let] the peace of God, which surpasses all understanding, . . . guard your hearts and minds" (Phil. 4:7, NKJV).

Examine the Scriptures and/or your answers in today's lesson. Determine the most meaningful thought for you today. Write your thought for the day here:

_____

_____

_____

Applying what God is pointing out to you is essential. How will you apply this truth to your life today? _____

_____

_____

Write a short prayer to God that summarizes your thoughts._____

_____

_____

_____

_____

Did God bring to mind someone who needs to hear this truth? Who?_____

_____

Thought for the Day:

I need to give my request to God, but trust the decision to Him.

◆

D A Y   F O U R

It is appointed for men to die once, but after this the judgment.
HEBREWS 9:27, NKJV

"For what is a man profited if he gains the whole world, and loses his own soul?"
MATTHEW 16:26, NKJV

Living and Dying

It was April 25, 1982. Eva and I were alone in her private hospital room as she battled cancer. She was lying in bed with her head propped up on pillows when I heard her weak little voice say, "Am I going to die?"

I was stunned and not prepared for her question. I have always been forthright with Eva, but I was greatly tempted to lie to her. After a long pause, I heard myself say, "Yes, you are going to die."

She said, "I'm scared."

I asked, "Why are you scared?"

She said, "Because I made a mess of my life."

How could she say such a thing? This lady who had traveled the world by my side, who was my stable companion, who kept encouraging me, who left a heritage to a host of women whom she helped to understand their role as wife and mother, and who was a faithful career mother?

I asked, "Why do you say this?"

Her answer was a complete surprise. "I could have been a better mother. I could have been more careful with the money. I could have been a better witness. I could have been more affectionate toward you."

How should I respond? I was always proud of the way she handled her role as a mother. It's true, she could have been more careful with money, but what did it matter now? There are very few women who served the Lord as she did. As far as being more affectionate toward me, only she would know.

My first impulse was to reassure her that she was wrong. But then I remembered many instances when, after listening to someone unburden themselves to us, we were tempted to soft-pedal their story. The only way to really help them was not to offer human sympathy, but to help them call sin by its right name.

These thoughts ran through my mind. Eva was about to meet Jesus. She wasn't concerned about her plants or her wardrobe or her makeup. She was concerned about her soul.

Finally I whispered, "You know what we would advise people who told us a story like that, don't you?"

She answered, "If you will confess your sins, He is faithful and just to forgive us our sins and to cleanse us from all unrighteousness" (1 John 1:9, NKJV).

She went on to tell the Lord what she told me. I could hardly hear her voice. As she prayed, it dawned on me that everything she said was true of me. I could have been a better father, more careful with the money, a better witness, more affectionate toward Eva.

When Eva finished her prayer, I prayed my prayer. Two weary pilgrims in a hospital room, getting our hearts cleaned up by the living God. I look back on that incident as one of the most inspiring, refreshing, renewing moments in our forty-two years of marriage. It was a final tune-up before the supreme event of all: preparing to meet the Lord.

The next day I was alone with Eva in her room. She was alert and seemed supernaturally peaceful.

I asked, "Are you scared today?"

She said, "No, not at all."

I asked, "Why not?"

She said, with a broad smile, "I got the garbage cleaned out of my heart last night."

I asked, "Are you ready to go?"

"Yes," she said.

Some visitors dropped in. When they left, I asked her if she would like to talk to our daughter Beth because our son Dick and his wife Patti had called the day before. I dialed the number and Eva chatted with Beth.

About a half hour later, Eva dozed off. I noticed that she was breathing unusually heavy. Just then, Sue, our daughter who was helping me take care of Eva, walked in. Together we watched Eva take a final breath and she was gone. I heard Sue say, "Praise the Lord." I agreed. What a wonderful experience. She was with the Lord whom we loved and served. "Precious in the sight of the Lord is the death of His saints" (Ps. 116:15, NKJV).

I cannot and could not look at her death as a tragedy. I suppose it all depends on your preparation, and we really believe that to meet Jesus was the ultimate, supreme event of life.

Recently, I talked to a couple who had not seen their son for four years because he was in another country, getting an education. Of course they missed him, but they would not for one moment deprive him of that privilege.

I look at Eva's death in the same way. What a privilege for her to go on ahead to meet Jesus. Of course we miss her, but we would not for one moment deprive her of that privilege.

There were piles of cards that arrived after Eva died. One stood out that came from Dr. Earl Radmacher, the president of Western Baptist Seminary:

"The Ship"

I am standing upon the seashore. A ship at my side spreads her sails to the morning breeze and starts for the blue ocean. She is an object of beauty and strength and I watch her until at length she hangs like a speck of white cloud just where the sea and sky come down to mingle with each other. Then someone at my side says, "There, she's gone."

"Gone where?" Gone from my sight . . . that is all. She is as large in mast and hull and spar as she was when she left my side, and just as able to bear her load of living freight to the place of destination. Her diminished size is in me, not in her; and just at that moment when someone at my side says, "there she's gone," there are other voices ready to take up the glad shout, "Here she comes!"

And that is dying.[1]

"Come you blessed of My Father, inherit the kingdom prepared for you from the foundation of the world" (Matt. 25:34, NKJV).

The key to anticipating the death of the people we know and love is *preparation.* When you love someone as much as you do the Lord and He calls that person to come to Him, you will be pleased with His decision. This is the ultimate, crowning event that all of us will experience if we meet the conditions. A warm welcome from the One who loves us is what we eagerly anticipate if our conscience is clear.

I later found a note among Eva's papers, dated January 10, 1982:

Through this experience I've had the joy and comfort of having my family and friends upholding me in prayer and supporting me in every way. This has given strength, relaxation, and a deep sense of comfort and peace; and to know God has been with me, near me, beside me, with the promise: "I will *never* leave thee nor forsake thee," what perfect peace and comfort this has been! Jesus had to suffer that awful experience of separation from *His Father,* He suffered alone, I have never experienced this!

She died April 26, 1982. "O death, where is thy sting? O grave, where is thy victory?" (1 Cor. 15:55, KJV).

Do you believe Eva experienced the peace of God? _____

Do you believe God will give you His peace in your crisis?_____

If you are going through a crisis, stop now and ask God for peace. If you are not currently in the midst of a crisis, take time to pray for a friend or family member.

Examine the Scriptures and/or your answers in today's lesson. Determine the most meaningful thought for you today. Write your thought for the day here:

_____

_____

_____

_____

Applying what God is pointing out to you is essential. How will you apply this truth to your life today? _____

_____

_____

Write a short prayer to God that summarizes your thoughts._____

_____

_____

_____

_____

Did God bring to mind someone who needs to hear this truth? Who?_____

_____

Thought for the Day:

A prepared heart has no fear of death and what lies beyond.

♦

DAY FIVE

Prepared for This World

Are most of us too busy to hear God's whispers; does it take a clap of thunder to get our attention?

> **"For what is a man profited if he gains the whole world and loses his own soul?"**
> MATTHEW 16:26, NKJV

Watching events unfold in my life and noting my responses to them have helped me draw some personal conclusions about this world.

> 1. **"You shall love the Lord your God with all your heart, with all your soul, and with all your mind."**
>
> **(Matthew 22:37, NKJV)**

This command was a puzzle to me for a long time. How can I tell how much I love God? Is loving God in conflict with loving my family? Then one day I received a very clear answer given by Jesus himself: "He who has My commandments and keeps them, it is he who loves Me" (John 14:21, NKJV).

If I love Him, I will study and obey His commandments as the single top priority of my life. Observing whether I am obeying Him is a quick check to see if I have a rebellious spirit. He said that to love God is the greatest commandment of them all.

One step in preparing to live in this world is checking to see how much you love God. On a scale of one to ten, place a mark as to where you believe your love for God exists today:

Where would you place yourself on a scale that conveyed your obedience to God?

How do they match up? How should they match up? _____

_____

_____

> **2. "You shall love your neighbor as yourself."**
>
> **(Matthew 22:39, NKJV)**

Jesus said that this is the second greatest commandment of them all and it is like the first. This commandment has two sides to it. Jesus said that I am to look after my own soul as a priority equal to loving God: "For what is a man profited if he gains the whole world, and loses his own soul?" (Matt. 16:26, NKJV).

The other side of the command is to love everyone and be as concerned about their souls as my own.

> **3. "The earth is the LORD's."**
>
> **(Psalm 24:1, NKJV)**

This fact has been a source of great freedom to me. I don't own anything. I am a steward of someone else's property. It belongs to the One I am to love with all my heart, soul, and mind. If I do, then I will care for His property as if it were my own. The Bible tells me that all that is in the world will be burned up. If that is true, then I need to heed the advice of my friend, Jack Klemke: to hold the things in the world lightly. It will all become an ash pile. Only people will be left!

> **4. "It is appointed for men to die once, but after this the judgment."**
>
> **(Hebrews 9:27, NKJV)**

This ought to be welcome, exciting news. Recently my wife, Jo, and I went to visit her ninety-nine-year-old mother-in-law. Jo eagerly looked forward to this visit. The closer we got, the more excited she got. Finally, Jo saw her: the crowning moment of a long journey to Salem, Oregon. What a pleasure to greet someone whom you love! Who would want to withhold such a privilege from anyone?

After meeting the Lord comes the judgment. If I have kept His commandments (the test of our love) then I can anticipate this greeting: "Come, you blessed of My Father, inherit the kingdom prepared for you from the foundation of the world" (Matt. 25:34, NKJV).

Happy thought!

Are you prepared to meet the Lord at the judgment?_____

Do you have friends or family that are not prepared to meet God? _____

_____

Take time to pray for them right now and ask God to give you an opportunity to share Christ with them.

> **5. "Precious in the sight of the LORD is the death of His saints."**
>
> **(Psalm 116:15, NKJV)**

The key to anticipating the death of the people I know and love is *preparation*. When I love someone as much as I love the Lord and He calls that person to come to

Him, I will be pleased with His decision, provided my conscience is clear toward that person. This is the crowning event for the people we love: a warm welcome from our Lord.

Are you prepared to meet God or to give up a family member or friend to God? _____

> **6. "Grow in the knowledge of the Lord and Savior Jesus Christ. To Him be the glory both now and forever."**
>
> **(2 Peter 3:18, NKJV)**

Preparation for meeting the God I care about is a happy task. As I prepare and wait, I remember these things:

- Grow in grace. The ultimate achievement in yielding to the grace of God is to become more gracious as I grow older.

- Grow in the knowledge of the Lord Jesus Christ. The more I study His commandments and do them, the more my appreciation of the benefits of obedience grows.

- Glorify Him, now and forever with my thoughts, emotions, and behavior. My decision to please God in these ways must be renewed day by day.

Examine the Scriptures and/or your answers in today's lesson. Determine the most meaningful thought for you today. Write your thought for the day here:

_____

_____

_____

_____

_____

Applying what God is pointing out to you is essential. How will you apply this truth to your life today? _____

_____

_____

Write a short prayer to God that summarizes your thoughts._____

_____

_____

_____

Did God bring to mind someone who needs to hear this truth? Who?_____

_____

Thought for the Day:

Preparing to meet God can be a happy task.

◆

(Optional—But Recommended!)

Bring forward your thoughts from each day:

1. _____
2. _____
3. _____
4. _____
5. _____

Bring forward your application:

1. _____
2. _____
3. _____
4. _____
5. _____

Bring forward your prayers:

1. _____
2. _____
3. _____
4. _____
5. _____

Bring forward who you shared your thoughts with:

1. _____

2. _____

3. _____

4. _____

5. _____

Thought for the Week:

Practicing these principles will produce a joyful life and take
the sting out of death.

◆

UNIT ELEVEN

I Prayed, but I Still
Didn't Feel Right

Thought Starter:

Why do you feel good after praying sometimes, and other times you
are anxious?

◆

Memory Verse for the Week:

**For the eyes of the LORD are on the righteous, and his ears are open
to their prayers.**
1 PETER 3:12, NKJV

DAY ONE

Be anxious for nothing, but in everything by prayer and supplication, with thanksgiving, let your requests be made known to God; and the peace of God, which surpasses all understanding, will guard your hearts and minds through Christ Jesus.
PHILIPPIANS 4:6–7, NKJV

The Need for Prayer

I was asked to speak to a group gathered for "a day of prayer." This was a good assignment because, like most speakers, I usually learned more in preparation for the presentation than the audience did in listening to the message. I spent three days thumbing through my Bible, reflecting and meditating on the subject of prayer.

Looking back, I did a lot of praying while Eva was struggling with cancer and also when my second wife, Marcey, died suddenly. I did a lot of praying before Jo and I married. There have been other crises in my life when I pleaded with God to help me solve a problem. But upon reflection, I have found that it is very easy to drift away from watching God work.

When do you find it easiest to rely on God, in the peaceful times or during a crisis? Explain your answer. _____

_____

_____

A day of prayer, or, more precisely, an annual day of prayer, served me well. It gave me a chance to pause, to let the world go by for a day, and to contemplate the privilege of talking things over with the Creator of the universe.

The verse at the head of this unit promises the peace that passes understanding will guard our hearts and minds as a by-product of prayer: a peace that is a quiet, still, calm, serene state of heart and mind. Everyone seeks this, but not everyone wants to meet the conditions. Prayer and supplication imply the acceptance of the truth that you must submissively and earnestly relinquish control over the events of your life to Someone else.

This proposition is a bit much for "modern" self-sufficient people who may have achieved an education, a position, wealth, power, or authority, without giving God a thought. Why should they turn control of their lives over to anyone, even God?

The answer is that sooner or later, a peaceful heart and mind will elude you. Personal attainment, competence, and intelligence are heady stuff, but not the keys to finding the peace of God. Truly self-sufficient people find this hard to believe.

I remember sitting across the desk from a businessman who had all the benefits of success: a large, beautifully decorated home located on spacious, well-tended grounds, a summer home, a farm, the finest food, clothing, cars, and the privilege of frequent travel to other countries. He achieved it on his own, yet now he was telling me how and why he needed the Lord.

He and his wife had been invited to attend an executive seminar a year earlier by several men whom he respected. On the way to the seminar, they rode in silence the whole three hours, nursing mutual hostility toward each other, in luxurious, air-conditioned comfort. They were utterly miserable; this was the third straight day they had not spoken to each other.

They sat in the audience and listened to other businessmen and their wives give their testimonies that they had achieved everything on their own except peace and contentment. Only when they turned control of their lives over to God were they able to experience the peace that passes understanding.

Can you remember a time when God provided for you peace and contentment that passed all understanding? What did you learn that you could share with others? _____

_____

Separately at the conference, both he and his wife prayed and turned control of their lives over to the Lord. This simple step added the missing link for them: access to the peace of God that passes understanding.

A statement once caught my attention. I wrote it down but failed to record the source: "It would seem that a good head, excellent vision, a strong heart, a strong body, an inexhaustible purse; you'd have it made."

Not so when it comes to finding peace of heart and mind. St. Augustine once said to God: "You made us for yourself, and our heart is restless until it finds rest in You."

Even Jesus, God's own Son, needed to turn His life over to God. When He was about to be crucified, He made a request to God: "Father, if it is Your will, remove this cup from Me; nevertheless not My will, but Yours, be done" (Luke 22:42, NKJV).

The answer was "no." Finishing the task was necessary. It seems that everyone takes his turn in enduring something he would rather not face.

Examine the Scriptures and/or your answers in today's lesson. Determine the most meaningful thought for you today. Write your thought for the day here:

_____

_____

_____

_____

Applying what God is pointing out to you is essential. How will you apply this truth to your life today? _____

_____

_____

Write a short prayer to God that summarizes your thoughts. _____

_____

_____

_____

_____

Did God bring to mind someone who needs to hear this truth? Who? _____

_____

Thought for the Day:

Everyone takes their turn in enduring something they would
rather not face.

♦

D A Y   T W O

The Method of Prayer

Jesus cautioned His disciples about just giving the appearance of praying to God: "When you pray, you shall not be like the hypocrites. For they love to pray standing in the synagogues and on the corners of streets, that they may be seen by men. Assuredly, I say to you, they have their reward" (Matt. 6:5–6, NKJV).

I am reminded of some lines in Shakespeare's *Hamlet:*

> My words fly up
> My thoughts remain below
> Words without thoughts
> Never to heaven go.[1]

I am ashamed to say it, but as I look back, I can recall instances when, as a part of an audience, I was asked to come to the platform to pray without any warning or preparation. On the way to the platform, I would pull together some random thoughts. I'd ask the audience to bow their heads to pray with me. Most of them would dutifully do so, and I'd speak some words. When finished, I could hardly remember what I had said. I doubt whether the audience did either. I'm not sure my words got beyond the ceiling.

What advice would you give a person if they said to you, "I pray but my words do not get beyond the ceiling!"_____

_____

_____

It's a simple matter to say, "Let us pray." It is equally simple to close our eyes and bow our heads. We can join a group for "a day of prayer." All this can be done without praying. Jesus once chided the scribes and Pharisees: "These people draw near to Me with their mouth, and honor Me with their lips, but their heart is far from Me" (Matt. 15:8, NKJV).

Praying is making our requests known to God. The decision regarding our requests is His. The evidence that you have really gotten through to God is that: "the peace of God that passes all understanding, will guard your heart and mind through Christ Jesus ." Then, you "watch God work."

Do you have difficulty watching God work after you pray, or do you have the ability to sit back and watch Him work?_____

When Eva was struggling with cancer, we both requested that she be healed. We both recognized that the decision was out of our hands. Close friends urged us to exercise faith. They said that the evidence of adequate faith was her healing.

Neither Eva nor I could accept that idea. To us, the evidence of faith was peace that passes understanding, guarding our hearts and minds through Jesus Christ. To us, it seemed presumptuous to tell God what to do. We make the request; God makes the decision. We needed to line up our requests with the will of the Creator.

A week before Eva died, one of our friends, a very sincere Christian, came by and said that as she was praying for Eva, the Lord clearly revealed to her that Eva could choose to live or die. If she chose life, she would need to endure some pain, but she could live.

A letter arrived at the same time from a precious friend, telling us that in prayer the Lord gave this person assurance that God would honor her prayer of faith and heal Eva.

What would you do if your friends had told you these things?_____

_____

What were we to do with these developments? Eva was getting weaker and weaker. Our response was to turn to the Bible: "If you abide in Me, and My words abide in you, you will ask what you desire, and it shall be done for you" (John 15:7, NKJV).

"If you ask anything in My name, I will do it. If you love Me, keep My commandments."
JOHN 14:14–15, NKJV

The effective, fervent prayer of a righteous man avails much.
JAMES 5:16, NKJV

Building yourselves up on your most holy faith, praying in the Holy Spirit.
JUDE 20, NKJV

The eyes of the LORD are on the righteous, and His ears are open to their prayers.
1 PETER 3:12, NKJV

The Bible tells us that effective praying implies familiarity with the commandments, obedience, and fervent, righteous walking in the Spirit by faith. That is difficult to measure up to. Eva and I decided that as best we could tell, we qualified to approach the Lord once more. We could not honestly say any more than what we had already said. Our prayer was that we agreed with our friends that Eva could live, but we wanted God's will.

Eva died.

Examine the Scriptures and/or your answers in today's lesson. Determine the most meaningful thought for you today. Write your thought for the day here:

_____

_____

_____

Applying what God is pointing out to you is essential. How will you apply this truth to your life today? _____

_____

Write a short prayer to God that summarizes your thoughts._____

_____

_____

_____

Did God bring to mind someone who needs to hear this truth? Who?_____

_____

Thought for the Day:

The peace that passes all understanding comes from prayer that is based on the Word of God.

♦

DAY THREE

The Evidence of Prayer
in Our Lives

During the time Eva struggled with cancer, another crisis was developing. I was involved in a real estate investment with a group of Christians. We united in prayer for the success of this venture. Without getting into the details, suffice it to say that the project was not doing well. The project went belly up and with it a great deal of my money.

What can you say? The conclusion I came to is contained in a Bible verse: "As the heavens are higher than the earth, so are My ways higher than your ways, and My thoughts than your thoughts" (Isa. 55:9, NKJV).

There were many, many people who were united in requesting that Eva should live. There were many people praying for the success of that business venture.

One must conclude that none of us were thinking God's thoughts, nor did our wishes fit with His ways. This requires all of us to search our hearts daily to be sure we qualify to speak in Jesus' name.

In *Chapel News*,² Knute Larson wrote on prayer, using a good visual aid that I feel helps explain our interaction with God in the area of prayer:

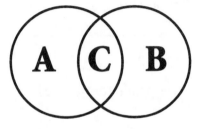

Two circles explain how prayer works in a simple way. "If you ask anything in my name, I will do it" (John 14:14, NKJV).

Area A is prayers we pray that are not answered, possibly because we ask selfishly. "And even when you do ask you don't get it because your whole aim is wrong—you want only what will give you pleasure." (James 4:3, LB, emphasis added).

Area B is where there are blessings or things God would do for us if we just asked. The Bible tells us why we don't have them: "The reason you don't have what you want is that you don't ask God for it" (James 4:2, LB).

Intersection C shows answered prayers in line with God's will.

I can recall some glib prayers that I have prayed, such as asking God to help me keep my priorities in order or to help me place my family and the things of this world in proper perspective. I've asked God to use my life and all that I have for His glory. If I expected any answers, I didn't expect the ones I received. But death and financial loss did get my attention. And my experience with prayer over the years has grown to recognize peace, the peace only God gives.

Examine the Scriptures and/or your answers in today's lesson. Determine the most meaningful thought for you today. Write your thought for the day here:

_____

_____

_____

Applying what God is pointing out to you is essential. How will you apply this truth to your life today? _____

_____

Write a short prayer to God that summarizes your thoughts._____

_____

_____

_____

Did God bring to mind someone who needs to hear this truth? Who?_____

_____

Thought for the Day:

The evidence that your prayer is acceptable to God is that you experience the peace of God in your heart.

♦

DAY FOUR

Thought Starter:

The key to joyful, peaceful, thankful living is to plan your day, put your trust in God, walk in the Spirit, and watch how the day turns out.

Rejoice always, pray without ceasing, in everything give thanks; for this is the will of God in Christ Jesus for you.
1 THESSALONIANS 5:16–18, NKJV

Rejoice Always

Many years ago, I renewed a commitment to serve the Lord as my top priority. I was reading Psalm 1 and the first word, *blessed,* caught my attention. What does that mean? The concordances and dictionaries that I consulted said that blessed means "cheerful, calmly happy, or well off." I knew I was a candidate for that. Verse 2 gave one characteristic of this blessed person: "His delight is in the law of the LORD; and in his law doth he meditate day and night" (Ps. 1:2, KJV).

That struck me as a very tall order in that the law of the Lord is contained in a very thick book called the Bible. And how does one meditate day and night?

What do you believe "meditate day and night" means?_____

_____

_____

At the time, it was basketball season and I loved basketball. I read about the game; I watched it, talked about it, and followed the careers of certain players. Basketball was well ingrained in the background of my thinking.

It was also very satisfying to play the game in my younger days. I memorized all the rules of basketball, because I couldn't play successfully if they were not part of my subconscious thinking. I didn't have time in the middle of a game to say, "Now, what was that rule about standing in the key too long?"

Living is like that also. If we wait until the actual event, God's laws governing that situation in life will not be part of our background thinking and we will often end up making a wrong decision. We need to be ready with God's law in our subconscious so we don't end up with regrets after the fact. If the law is to be in the background of our thinking, we must first of all have portions of it in our minds.

Since memorizing is not one of my strengths, I looked for an easy verse to get started with: "Rejoice always" (1 Thess. 5:16, NKJV).

My goal was to spend two weeks with this verse in the background of my thinking. This meant that "joy, delight, great gladness, emotion of keen or lively pleasure arising from present or expected good" needed to be in me always.

Always? These were my first responses: You've got to be kidding. Who wants to be that joyful? Should anyone be that joyful? Is it even appropriate? What about a death in the family? Discovery that a child is on drugs? Your partner is in an adulterous relationship? Job loss? Investment wiped out? Addressed rudely? Injured in an accident? Neglected or criticized? Beaten or abused?

You can add to this list. Life doesn't happen the way you want it to.

While thinking about this verse over a period of two weeks, I did not succeed once in rejoicing for a full twenty-four hour period. One day during this period, I was disgusted and dreading the day even before I got out of bed. (Have you ever awakened in the morning saying, "Oh, no, I woke up! Must I get out of bed?")

Can one enjoy facing a crisis? I've often thought that joy is on the other side of a difficult problem and that joy only comes with a solution. This verse suggested, however, that one can joyfully work toward a solution.

I concluded that this is not humanly possible. To rejoice always requires a miracle: not just an ordinary one, but a full-blown, supernatural miracle.

The Bible says that joy is a fruit of the Spirit of God (Gal. 5:22). This is a condition of the heart that occurs at any given time when one consciously recognizes the impossibility of human achievement of joy, and as an act of the will, yields to the joy of the Lord. The miracle then follows.

Do you need the fruit of the Spirit of God today to give you the right perspective on a difficult situation? If so, stop now and pray. Ask God to control you with His Spirit and give you a supernatural miracle of joy. _____

_____

_____

_____

My friend, Sue, lived in Nairobi, East Africa, when she received word that her brother had died suddenly. She decided to go to California to be with her sister-in-law and attend a memorial service for him. The trip from Nairobi to Los Angeles was a long, demanding journey, and she realized that if she ever needed peace and joy, it was now.

As she started out on her long journey, she prayed for the fruit of the Spirit, peace and joy, to be her companion.

It was an uneventful trip until she arrived in Dallas. The flight from Dallas to Los Angeles was overbooked and she found herself on the waiting list. One by one names were called and she watched the passengers go on board.

It occurred to her that she might not get on this flight, which meant she would miss the memorial service. Because she had prayed that she would get there in time for the service, it never occurred to her that she would miss it after traveling ten thousand miles. The thought crept into her mind that if she were to enjoy this moment, it would have to be in Dallas, wait-listed, and likely to miss the plane.

In fact, she did miss the plane. Only a miracle could give her joy in her heart in this situation, and she needed it now more than ever. At this point she could enjoy making the best of the predicament, or she could be unhappy and bitter. Either way, she was stuck in Dallas.

She chose to ask the Lord to fill her with His joy and God responded to her request. She has the same option every day. We all do.

Examine the Scriptures and/or your answers in today's lesson. Determine the most meaningful thought for you today. Write your thought for the day here:

_____

_____

_____

_____

Applying what God is pointing out to you is essential. How will you apply this truth to your life today? _____

_____

_____

*Write a short prayer to God that summarizes your thoughts.*_____

_____

_____

_____

_____

_____

Did God bring to mind someone who needs to hear this truth? Who?_____

_____

Thought for the Day:
Rejoicing always only works when you let God do the work.

◆

DAY FIVE

Pray Without Ceasing

Many people have never experienced the fun of turning everything over to God and letting Him control the situation.

The second verse I chose to work on was a bit more difficult; three words: "Pray without ceasing" (1 Thess. 5:17, NKJV).

A friend was driving me to the Atlanta airport. I was sharing with him my experience with the verse, "Pray without ceasing" plus "Rejoice always." It was 4:00 P.M. and up to then I had enjoyed the day. It had turned out as I had prayed.

We arrived at the airport early, so we sat in the car and talked a while. I said good-bye to my friend, entered the airport, and presented my ticket to the attendant at the desk. My destination was Asheville, where I was to speak at a nearby conference center that night. The attendant informed me that the flight had just left, and there were no more flights to Asheville until morning. I was stunned. My watch said there was plenty of time: my watch had stopped!

How would you respond in the situation? _____

_____

_____

What help could you give someone else that is in this situation? _____

_____

_____

_____

I quickly called the center in Asheville and told them what had happened. They had already dispatched a driver to drive sixty miles to pick me up: He would surely need some joy when he discovered I wasn't there. And as for me, I ended up praying and rejoicing all alone in a motel room in Atlanta.

The evening alone was enjoyable. God gave me no clue as to why this happened. He was silent. Yet, this was a rare day when I trusted and rejoiced all day.

The next morning I was at the airport bright and early. The plane was scheduled to arrive in time for me to easily make my speech in Asheville at 11:00 A.M. As I waited for the plane to load, I rehearsed my two Bible verses: "Rejoice always" plus "Pray without ceasing." The plane was full and took off on time. It was only a half-hour flight, and soon we felt the plane head downward. What a good feeling. Then we felt the plane head up again. The speaker system came on: "This is the captain speaking. I regret to tell you that there is fog in Asheville; we are proceeding to land in Johnson City."

With that announcement, one could hear murmuring throughout the airplane. Most of the polite, nicely dressed passengers became visibly unhappy. One well-groomed man bawled out the flight attendant because there was fog in Asheville.

I was rehearsing my verses and, strangely enough, contentedly watching God work. We landed in Johnson City. Our plane load of mostly disgusted passengers descended on a hapless ticket agent behind the counter who had just heard the bad news himself. One nice-looking man banged his fist on the counter and moaned, "I want to get to Asheville."

As for me, I ran to a phone to call the Center to tell them I wouldn't be there at 11:00 A.M. Unfortunately, the poor driver who went to meet me last night had already left for the Asheville airport. For the second time, the conference director had no speaker. The men at the Conference Center and the driver needed a good supply of trust and joy for this day also.

Meanwhile, Henry Brandt was rehearsing his verses: "Pray without ceasing" plus "Rejoice always." The ticket agent behind the counter looked quite harried. I felt sorry for him, so I went up to him and told him I was also a passenger. I encouraged him to process me last and I would hover in the background and give him moral support. He looked at me as though I was drunk. What was a cheerful, relaxed, supportive person doing here?

It took an hour and a half for the agent to line up micro-busses to transport us to Asheville. One by one the busses left with a load of disgruntled passengers. I was the only one left. He motioned me forward and said, "I'm sorry, I'm out of busses. But I do have a limousine out there and if you don't mind, I will send you to Asheville in it." "I don't mind," I said. We went outside and there sat a long, black Chrysler limousine. I sat in the back seat and motioned the chauffeur to proceed. Soon we caught up to the first bus. I waved happily as we passed.

That is the way it goes. Sometimes the day turns out as we had planned. Often it doesn't.

Prayer is just talking to God with our mouth or with our heart. How is it possible to pray without ceasing? Does this mean that one stops doing everything else and just continuously talks to God? What would you talk about? Do you ignore your family and friends? What about going to work and interacting with the people there? Going shopping? Going visiting? This verse surely can't mean what it says.

What do you believe this verse means, "pray without ceasing"?_____

_____

_____

I can commit my day into God's hands. I can tell him what I want to have happen. I can compare what happens with what my requests were. Then whatever happens, I can depend on a living God to look after me and I can trust Him to give me a day's supply of joy. Life may not always make sense, but I can always trust Him.

It is never dull talking with God, because his plans are always different and better than ours: "This plan of mine is not what you would work out, neither are my thoughts the same as yours! For just as the heavens are higher than the earth, so are my ways higher than yours, and my thoughts than yours" (Isa. 55:8–9, TLB).

The third verse I chose to work on had four words in it: In everything give thanks" (1 Thess. 5:18, NKJV).

In everything? When the car won't start? Tire is flat? Your partner is fifteen minutes late? You are being ignored at home?

I was asked to speak in Mombassa, a city on Kenya's Indian Ocean coast. My sponsor and his wife were named Justice and Jemima. They met me at the airport and seemed to glow with appreciation as we greeted each other. As we drove toward the hotel, he remarked that he was so thankful that a friend from another mission had loaned them this car. Justice's car was broken down and he could not afford to fix it.

He was pleased to tell me that a local Baptist congregation had made their church auditorium available. It was the best location in town, easily accessible from all directions. He added that very few people owned cars, so they must get where they're going by bus.

About one hundred and fifty people were already there. The mood of the people before the meeting was congenial and friendly. The host pastor received us gladly. Justice was elated at the turnout, for the response was beyond his expectations. The audience's reception of the material was positive. Many of them approached me to express their thanks for my coming. I might add that the meeting was from 5:00 P.M. to 6:30 P.M. so those in attendance could catch their buses before dark.

For this to make any sense to you, some background information might help. Outside, it was about 110 degrees. The humidity was as high as it could get. The church was located on as busy a corner as you could imagine and was also on a heavy truck route. When the signal light on the corner changed, the trucks revved up their engines to get going again. Cars tooted their horns frequently.

When the church was built ten years before, this was a quiet spot. The business area of the city grew in that direction, and now the church is surrounded by buildings, with the heavy traffic going by.

With no air-conditioning, all doors and windows were wide open to catch any movement of air that might relieve the intense heat and humidity. As I spoke to the people, the sweat poured down my face, into my eyes, and downward all over my body. The faces of people in the audience glistened with sweat. The church's public address system was turned as high as possible above the roar of the heavy traffic.

Next door was a Moslem temple. At 6:00 P.M. their public address system issued a call to prayer that could be heard for blocks. For a minute and a half, I had to compete with a Moslem call to prayer.

What would be your response to meeting in a location like this?
❑ Why don't they get some air-conditioning in this place?
❑ It is just too hot to really worship in this place.
❑ I can't hear the speaker well enough to get anything out of this message.
❑ I am so glad that God allows us to meet together as Christians.

All this bedlam around us, and in this setting dozens of people expressed their thanks for a convenient location and a public address system that was louder than the traffic noise.

These people taught me that one can have a grateful, thankful heart in a setting where the body is struggling with heat and high humidity, where the eardrums are taxed to the limit trying to block out deafening noise and at the same time trying to listen to a speaker. Here, funds are limited and clothing is scarce. Medical attention is almost nonexistent, education hard to come by; money is precious. Housing is substandard according to our definition.

None of these conditions kept these people from turning their hearts God-ward and opening their ears to hear from Him. If they were to have hearts filled with gratitude and appreciation and thankfulness on this day, it had to be under present conditions. They could be discontentedly complaining about the present and dwell on what might have been or what could be in the future.

Many Christians struggle with having an ungrateful spirit. How do you relate to God concerning gratitude? Do you find yourself thanking and praising God for your present conditions? Read Ephesians 5:19–20. According to this passage of Scripture, how often and for what are you to give thanks:

❏ Whenever you think about it.
❏ In every circumstance of every day.
❏ Only when you give a testimony to someone else.

Surely these people would like a better life-style. They work toward improvement like anyone else. As I think about them, I am reminded of these words: "A truly spirited Christian is a paradox in that he is always satisfied, yet ever seeking. He never thirsts, yet is always thirsting. He is perfectly content, yet always wanting more. He enjoys to the full what he possesses but knows there is more beyond and eagerly longs for it."[3]

The famous prayer of St. Francis of Assisi has inspired many of us:

> God, grant me the serenity
> To accept the things I cannot change,
> Courage to change the things I can,
> And wisdom to know the difference.

I have had wealthy clients who are very discontent that they don't have more. Then there are those like my friends in Kenya that are so thankful for very simple things. Our response of trust to God in terms of what we have is an excellent indicator of our walk with God.

I have seen in my own life that I need to stand with open hands before God. He can put into my hand or He can take out of my hand whatever He wants. This includes loved ones, finances, possessions, health, or anything. Sometimes it is painful, but I know He loves me and I can trust Him.

God loves us and wants our hearts to be satisfied with Him: "I have learned the secret of contentment in every situation, whether it be a full stomach or hunger, plenty or want; for I can do everything God asks me to with the help of Christ who gives me the strength and power" (Phil. 4:12–13, TLB).

He also wants us to appreciate everything that He has given us now, even the difficulties, because they are there for a purpose that is for our good: "In everything give thanks; for this is the will of God in Christ Jesus for you" (1 Thess. 5:18, NKJV).

Examine the Scriptures and/or your answers in today's lesson. Determine the most meaningful thought for you today. Write your thought for the day here:

_____

_____

_____

_____

Applying what God is pointing out to you is essential. How will you apply this truth to your life today? _____

_____

_____

Write a short prayer to God that summarizes your thoughts._____

_____

_____

_____

_____

_____

Did God bring to mind someone who needs to hear this truth? Who?_____

_____

Thought for the Day:

When we allow God to work out His plan for our lives, joy and thanksgiving will be present in our hearts.

◆

(Optional—But Recommended!)

Bring forward your thoughts from each day:

1. _____
2. _____
3. _____
4. _____
5. _____

Bring forward your application:

1. _____
2. _____
3. _____
4. _____
5. _____

Bring forward your prayers:

1. _____
2. _____
3. _____
4. _____
5. _____

Bring forward who you shared your thoughts with:

1. _____
2. _____
3. _____
4. _____
5. _____

Thought for the Week:

Talking with God produces opportunities to watch Him work His plan in our lives!

♦

UNIT TWELVE

If You Don't Want to, You Aren't Going To

Thought Starter:

Are your decisions in life made on the basis of whom you are trying to please?

♦

Memory Verse for the Week:

I beseech you therefore, brethren, by the mercies of God, that you present your bodies a living sacrifice, holy, acceptable to God, which is your reasonable service. And do not be conformed to this world, but be transformed by the renewing of your mind, that you may prove what is that good and acceptable and perfect will of God.

ROMANS 12:1–2, NKJV

217

DAY ONE

Now may the God of peace . . . make you complete in every good work to
do His will, working in you what is well pleasing in His sight, through Jesus
Christ, to whom be glory forever and ever.
HEBREWS 13:20–21, NKJV

Standards of Performance

In my high school days we had a basketball coach whom I both appreciated and
feared. When he was looking my direction I always tried to be shooting a basket,
which was the strong part of my game. When he walked toward me, however, I knew
what was coming.

"Good shot, Brandt," he would say. "Now let me see you dribble."

That was the worst part of my game. I hated to dribble, but he forced me to do
it. As a result I became a better player.

Every day during the 1988 Olympics, we heard and read about the years of sacrifice, hard work, and continuous training to which the athletes subjected themselves.
There was daily talk about world record holders. The standard of performance
included many comments on perfection: perfect physical condition, perfect weight,
perfect skill and performance, perfect attitude, perfect concentration, perfect persis-
tence in the face of competition or adversity, perfect teamwork if it was a team effort.

A few achieved perfection; no one can maintain it. Yet, athletes keep trying.

One heart-warming story that came out of those Olympics was about Jackie
Joyner Kersee, who competed in the heptathalon, a two-day series of seven events for
women. She grew up on Piggot Avenue in St. Louis, across the street from a tavern,
down the block from a pool hall, and around the corner from a playground.

"I knew at the age of nine that I could jump," she recalls. "That's when I started running and jumping off the porch."

A fireman's brigade of siblings used a potato chip bag to "borrow" sand from the playground and install a landing pit off the porch.

Nino Fennoy, a saintly coach of the kind these neighborhoods seem to inspire, steered her through a series of Junior Olympic championships and a busy career of basketball and volleyball at Lincoln High. The girls basketball team went 62-2 during her last two years, and Jackie was All-State. She went on to U.C.L.A. on a basketball scholarship and was a star performer there, too.

In 1981, Mary, her mother, who was the determined disciplinarian with a willow switch, died at age thirty-eight after a one-day illness. "Her determination," Jackie says, "passed to me."

Working under a U.C.L.A. assistant track coach, Bob Kersee, Jackie headed toward the 1984 games. She won a silver medal. She married her coach in 1986 and with his help, she overwhelmed the international field with the only 7,000-point performances (four of them) on record. In 1988, she took the gold medal. Jumping, she says, is like leaping for joy. "I don't know what it is about that extra second or inch." She always aches but never minds it. "To ask my body not to ache would be too much," she says.[1]

People helped her reach her goals in spite of the obstacles, but the desire, will, and drive had to come from her.

As I thought about this area of athletes and the Olympic atmosphere of striving for excellence, I recalled the struggles my wife and I experienced in the early years of our Christian life. We presented our bodies to God as a living sacrifice. We wanted our lives to be well pleasing in God's sight. We didn't have the foggiest idea of what such a commitment meant or how to go about discovering "that good and acceptable and perfect will of God." There was no well-marked highway. There was no two-way direct communication with God. We had a lot to learn.

Our faith in God and in the Bible as the Word of God was very shaky. We needed some exercise so we could improve and perfect our faith and hope in God. We decided that we needed to study the Bible first of all. Then we needed to test it against life. We also needed some teachers and coaches to help us along the way. But the desire and will to study, to improve, had to come from us.

How often do you currently read or study the Bible?

- ☑ Daily.
- ❑ Every other day.
- ❑ Once a week.
- ❑ Whenever I think about it.
- ❑ Almost never.

What do you need to improve your current devotion to reading the Word of God? _I read in the morning, but I need to re-check and extend what I read in the afternoon_

A young pastor, Dick Wilkenson, took an interest in us. He encouraged us to get a concordance and learn to use it. It would help us get biblical answers to our many questions, he said. We took his advice, which proved to be one of the most helpful moves we made to get to know what "pleasing God" meant.

It was he who introduced us to a biblical principle that disturbed us: "Seek first the kingdom of God and His righteousness, and all these things shall be added to you" (Matt. 6:33, NKJV).

Is there any other person, place, possession, or purpose in your life that takes first place over the kingdom of God? Make a list of those things that need to be moved out of first place. _Worry, clutter, self ambition, + restlessness_

Up to this point in my life, my main preoccupation was in acquiring a home and the means to assure a comfortable, secure life. We had a new car, a new house, membership in a sailing club, a sailboat, access to a golf and tennis club. Even thinking about God was not a serious consideration. My pastor kept bringing up this verse and urging us to review our priorities.

Sunday was the best time for sailing and doing homework. (I was taking some engineering courses at night.) Golf or tennis took two or three evenings. Looking after the lawn, playing with the children, visiting our families took up time. It seemed our world consisted of pleasing ourselves.

Does your world consist of pleasing yourself? _Not really, it consists with Keeping up with necessary pleasures from work + home_

What consumes your time through the week? _Work and related obligations - meetings, phone calls, supplies for TMS - Travel to + fro, 2 exercise classes, talking to friends_

Do you need some coaching along the way while dealing with making God's kingdom first? _Yes_

Examine the Scriptures and/or your answers in today's lesson. Determine the most meaningful thought for you today. Write your thought for the day here:

Hebrews 13; 20 - For God himself to work what is pleasing in his sight in me - and to rest in Him, this God of Peace

Applying what God is pointing out to you is essential. How will you apply this truth to your life today? *On this particular day — I will earnestly ask God to turn me from any sin, to direct my path, to protect my future. I will worship God in quietness.*

Write a short prayer to God that summarizes your thoughts. *Dear Holy Father, Provide me with clearer sight for the choices and paths moment by moment that please you. Let me know your Peace and Strength. Give me dicipline enough to acomplish my daily task. Let me have a greater more real knowledge of your presence + Help.*

Did God bring to mind someone who needs to hear this truth? Who? *Charlotte + Tony + Janet Guardiani also my son.*

Thought for the Day:

"Seek first the kingdom of God and His righteousness, and all these things will be added to you."

◆

DAY TWO

Training Requires Diligence

He kept asking us pesky questions in relation to that verse, such as: What are you doing with your time? What are you doing with your money? What are you studying in the Bible? Why weren't you in church on Sunday?

I had mixed feelings about him and his questions because I was embarrassed by the answers I had to give him.

Once, in exasperation, I told him to mind his own business. He said he was. As long as I came to his church, I was his business. He was my "coach."

Does your pastor or Bible teacher "mind your business?" _____

Gradually, our focus changed from things to people. People appeared from nowhere asking for help with their problems, and we would invite them to come for dinner. We discovered that these dinner invitations were very expensive.

Besides, we had very little background for helping people.

We started going to church regularly on Sundays. Our sailboat, golf clubs, and tennis racquets got less and less use.

For two years, 1942 to 1944, Eva and I struggled with that verse. What should come first in the use of our time, talent, and treasure? Both of us had a growing desire to know more about the Bible and to be of service to other people. Our thoughts went so far as to consider going back to college for a few years to study the Bible.

We reasoned that if the Bible contained the most important information in the world, we should know more about it.

How familiar are you with the Word of God?
☐ Vaguely.
☑ Well-read.
☐ Not very familiar.
☑ I need more study, but I do read and study the Bible consistently.

Have you placed enough of the Scripture in your heart for God to help you fight sin? *Yes, God brings verses and passages to mind, I still wish to truly learn more.*

Read Psalm 119:11. Does God want you to hide His Word in your heart? Why?

His word securely and permanently placed in your mind and heart will deter those choices that are against God.

Finally, my wife and I decided to test that verse. I compiled a financial statement that included everything we owned in the world. Then my wife and I sat down at the kitchen table and had an imaginary meeting with God. Eva and I showed God what we were worth and told Him we were prepared to risk it all in order to test this verse. We admitted that our minds were filled with doubts, but by faith we would try to obey God as a first priority. We reminded God that we were interested in the whole verse.

We told the young pastor about the step that we took, and we were considering returning to college. What did he think? He replied that this was a serious matter. I had a wife and two children, a one-year-old and a three-year-old. I was just getting a good start in the engineering field. He could not advise us one way or another. He said we would need to take a step of faith, and one test would be that we should have peace about such a move.

We had to admit that the whole idea scared us, and we were very uneasy about such thoughts. Our minds were filled with doubt, but we did want to obey God as a top priority. We asked God to give us some sign that we were thinking straight. We were very young Christians and were just learning what it meant to walk by faith, and faith doesn't require signs in order to move ahead.

When you are seeking an answer from God, does your faith require a sign?

We shared our thoughts with our parents and some trusted friends. They were all in agreement that we would be making a serious blunder.

The desire to know more about the Bible persisted. Should we abide by the judgment of our parents and friends? We asked God that question. His answer?

Silence.

Our pastor referred us to two Bible verses for our consideration as backup for his previous advice. We had to exercise our faith and yet be at ease about any move we made.

Without faith it is impossible to please Him, for he who comes to God must believe that He is, and that He is a rewarder of those who diligently seek Him.

HEBREWS 11:6, NKJV

May the God of hope fill you with all joy and peace in believing, that you may abound in hope by the power of the Holy Spirit.

ROMANS 15:13, NKJV

This verse in Romans is one of my favorite Bible verses, and if I understand it correctly, hope is entwined with joy and peace. These are the fruit of the Spirit. So we can hope, or expect, to handle the circumstances that come our way with an inner calm, free from agitation, untroubled by conflict or commotion.

The more we thought about expanding our biblical knowledge and serving people, the better we liked the idea and we became excited about going back to college. To do this meant that we had to sell the house and the boat. We could then finance two to three years of study time.

Again we asked God for a sign. His answer?

Silence.

Have you ever asked God for a sign and He answered by being completely silent? _____

Examine the Scriptures and/or your answers in today's lesson. Determine the most meaningful thought for you today. Write your thought for the day here:

_____

_____

_____

_____

Applying what God is pointing out to you is essential. How will you apply this truth to your life today? _____

_____

_____

Write a short prayer to God that summarizes your thoughts._____

_____

_____

_____

_____

Did God bring to mind someone who needs to hear this truth? Who?_____

_____

Thought for the Day:

Diligent application of God's Word will keep you on the right track
when you are learning about faith.

◆

D A Y   T H R E E

Running the Race

We decided to sell the house and the boat. All of our friends just shook their heads at our folly. Even the young pastor expressed doubts about our decision. It was 1944. As it turned out, we spent three of perhaps the most important years of our lives at Houghton College. It was there that we met many hundreds of fellow Christians who were also exercising their faith, studying to understand the Bible, and learning to live joyful, peaceful lives.

This experience sounds like a contradiction. On the one hand, my wife and I benefited greatly from the teachers, pastors, and friends we made along the way. On the other hand, there were times when we had to go it alone by faith in a loving God.

Can you remember times when you had to "go it" all alone by faith in a loving God? What did you learn from that situation? _____

_____

_____

The Olympic atmosphere is the same. The athletes strive diligently to develop minds and bodies. Preparation involves following the advice of teachers and coaches. But when the race is run, the athlete must go it alone and draw on past training and experience. Hopefully, the time of preparation will enable the athlete to perform better than ever before in the actual event. Everyone realizes that present performance is a compound of continuous preparation plus drawing on past experience. Even then, perfection is an illusive goal.

There is always a chance to start over when you fall on your face. The person that wants to improve works on developing and maintaining a wholesome personal life. A person needs some biblical principles and some teachers and coaches who will help him locate himself and guide him along the way. No one can maintain perfection, to be sure, but everyone can point toward perfection and work on getting closer.

When an athlete enters a contest that requires physical strength, he must have built up strength before the event. It's too late to start it when the contest begins. Practicing faith is also an exercise. It builds confidence in God just as surely as physical exercise builds muscle. This faith in God must be built up before a crisis, just like muscles must be built up before an event.

We were in for a surprise.

It was in January 1947, that a professor at Houghton College challenged me to go on for a master's degree in clinical psychology. I prayed and told God that I would want the best training available if that was the direction we should go. I asked Him to allow me to go to one of three universities that had what I believed to be good programs: University of Michigan, University of Minnesota, and University of Chicago. I also reminded God that my financial resources were dwindling and I was trusting Him to show me what to do about it. All three universities turned me down. In asking God for an explanation, His answer?

Silence.

What kind of explanation would you have given Dr. Brandt? _____

_____

I had received several good job offers, but it seemed to me that it made more sense to continue my education. From January through August I made many attempts to get God's attention for some specific guidance. I yelled at Him and expressed my anger and disgust at what I perceived to be his lack of attention to my problems. I even threatened to turn my back on Him and to tell people how He had treated me as I pouted for a while. His answer?

Silence.

Have any attempts to perfect your relationship with God left you confused? Write a testimony from your life that could be shared with others. _____

_____

_____

In August I moved my family to Detroit, my home town, and temporarily moved in with my folks. There was a new school in Detroit, Wayne University, that met in a condemned high school building. Reluctantly, I contacted the head of the clinical psychology department. He looked at my transcripts and commented that he did not like the Bible courses listed there, but he finally said that I could study at Wayne on academic probation for the first year. When I paid my tuition, I had exactly one dime left to my name, a wife, and three children. I flipped the dime into the air with my thumb, caught it with the same hand and crossed the street to buy a Coke.

"That's what I get for putting my faith in You," I prayed. "I'm broke, on probation, and in a dump of a school." God's answer? You guessed it.

Silence.

One of the biblical principles that I had been depending on was that if we put the Kingdom of God and His righteousness first, all these things will be added to us. To my mind, I had kept my end of the bargain. Right then it seemed to me that God had not kept His side of the deal.

My first class at Wayne State was in test administration. The professor paired us up in groups of two. We were to take a test and see which one of us could do it faster. My partner, Bill, was a dull, sleepy-looking person who didn't seem very bright. I beat him easily. I was getting more disgusted by the minute. He asked me my name and what I did. Reluctantly, I told him, "Nothing." Disinterested, I asked him the same questions. He said he was the head of the Psychology Department at General Motors Institute. I thought to myself, "Yea, yea, what a big liar. This guy couldn't head up sharpening the pencils at General Motors." He asked me, "Do you want a job?"

"Huh! Do I want a job?"

It turned out he *really* was what he said he was. In a matter of weeks I was teaching in the psychology department at General Motors Institute. In addition to a job, one of my benefits included a new Pontiac car, when cars after World War II were as scarce as hen's teeth. In addition, all my tuition was paid to work on a master's degree.

I told Bill, my new boss and angel, that all this was an answer to prayer. He replied, "The *heck* it is! I'm an atheist. I needed a teacher and you're qualified."

Examine the Scriptures and/or your answers in today's lesson. Determine the most meaningful thought for you today. Write your thought for the day here:

_____

_____

_____

_____

_____

Applying what God is pointing out to you is essential. How will you apply this truth to your life today? _____

_____

_____

Write a short prayer to God that summarizes your thoughts._____

_____

_____

_____

_____

Did God bring to mind someone who needs to hear this truth? Who?_____

_____

Thought for the Day:

Faith in God should be built up before a crisis occurs.

◆

D A Y   F O U R

God Is Faithful

After teaching there for six months, my boss asked me to prepare some courses in marriage and the family for General Motors engineers, because the company realized that an engineer couldn't work at his best level if problems in his marriage and family were on his mind. He told me I could consult with any sources anywhere in the world. This assignment gave me instant credibility with people that I contacted and the opportunity to learn from some of the finest teachers in the world, which was just exactly what I had asked God to do for me. Some of these teachers, with whom I came into contact during this project, later opened doors for me to study for a Ph.D. degree at Cornell University. He knew better than I where to get the finest training.

Once more, I learned that God is faithful. We can trust Him. Although God is sometimes silent, that never means He is not there.

I also believe God let my bank account dwindle to nothing because I really did not trust Him. At the time I wouldn't admit, even to myself, that I didn't really trust God. He waited until I was totally out of my own funds before He stepped in. He let me know that He could replenish my funds in His way and in His time.

Again, I asked God why He didn't explain to me what He was doing. His answer? Silence . . . but things were happening during His silence.

This experience helped me put my faith in the power of God. Perfect faith? Perhaps a few people attain it; the rest of us can work toward it.

As I look back over the years, I see that developing a real faith in our living God is one of the most important pillars that has sustained me. The events of life raised many unanswered questions. God was silent over and over again for long periods of time, even years, when I thought He should speak. There was sickness, death, financial problems, dishonesty, deception, and on and on. I wasn't exempt. When God was silent, I often looked to human wisdom or human sympathy, which were both readily available.

The Bible says: "All things work together for good to those who love God, to those who are called according to His purpose" (Rom. 8:28, NKJV).

We rest in this hope as we yield our lives daily to God by faith and as we experience the Holy Spirit's control of our responses. If, for whatever reason, we turn away from a daily yielding of our hearts to the Holy Spirit, we begin to think or say things such as: Why me? Why am I being singled out? Is God punishing me? That's what I get for trusting God. It's not fair. What's the use? Nothing turns out right.

*What would you suggest a Christian should do when they begin to ask these kinds of questions?*_____

_____

_____

These hopeless statements and questions are like a warning light on the dashboard of a car. It's time to stop as quickly as possible and find out what went wrong.

The hopeful person will calmly wait to see how things turn out. This picture in the Bible of a hopeful person is entwined with faith, peace, and love:

> Therefore, having been justified by faith, we have peace with God through our Lord Jesus Christ, through whom also we have access by faith into this grace in which we stand, and rejoice in hope of the glory of God. And not only that, but we also glory in tribulations, knowing that tribulation produces perseverance; and perseverance, character; and character, hope. Now hope does not disappoint, because the love of God has been poured out in our hearts by the Holy Spirit who was given to us.
>
> ROMANS 5:1–5, NKJV

If we put the Bible passages of Romans 5:1–5, Romans 15:13, and Hebrews 11:6 together, they tell us that walking with hope and faith while experiencing difficult times in life produces perseverance, character, love, joy, and peace.

But tough times do not always produce perseverance, character, and hope; it only happens when we put our faith in the Lord. Turning away from the Lord produces hopelessness, anxiety, worry, anger, and rebellion. If that is our position, we do not benefit from experience; we only suffer when we go through it alone.

My first attempts at helping people go back nearly fifty years to 1942. Since that time, I've listened to many stories of people's problems. Pain, death, financial loss, personal inner struggle, family struggles, interpersonal struggles: no matter what the problem was, each one was resolved sooner or later, one way or another.

The way a person approaches problems depends greatly on whether he is hopeful or hopeless and whether or not the person is familiar with the work of the Holy Spirit. It also depends on whom you seek to please, and often our faith is illogical to bystanders in our world.

When a person is in the middle of a problem it is usually a major issue to that person. I've watched people who are as frightened over a minor scratch as others who underwent major surgery. I observed someone create as much of a tense, anxious emergency over a missing dog as came from another person's son missing in combat. I watched someone become as uptight over buying a toaster as others over purchasing a house. I watched someone get as upset over losing a car key as did another person whose car was stolen.

Response to the trouble that comes our way on any day will reveal our spirit, not cause it. If we fail to respond by faith and hope, we can always start over again. No one is perfect. God understands us and deals with us where we are now. The Bible says: "There is none righteous, no, not one" (Rom. 3:10, NKJV).

We can't change our past failures, but God will forgive us of those sins if we ask Him. But, all of us can let the Holy Spirit control our lives today and in the future. This hopeful opportunity can be a pleasant, stimulating experience. God has made us to improve our performance and to enjoy the process; in the middle of the process, we can see His loving plans come together in His timing.

Examine the Scriptures and/or your answers in today's lesson. Determine the most meaningful thought for you today. Write your thought for the day here:

_____

_____

_____

_____

Applying what God is pointing out to you is essential. How will you apply this truth to your life today? _____

_____

Write a short prayer to God that summarizes your thoughts._____

_____

_____

_____

_____

Did God bring to mind someone who needs to hear this truth? Who?_____

_____

Thought for the Day:

God is faithful, loving, and forgiving of the past; we can trust him to train us for life.

◆

DAY FIVE

Getting Started in Biblical Foundations

Do you know that everyone can finish the race of life as a winner?

In a race, everyone runs but only one person gets first prize. So run your race to win. To win the contest you must deny yourselves many things that would keep you from doing your best. An athlete goes to all this trouble just to win a blue ribbon or a silver cup, but we do it for a heavenly reward that never disappears. So I run straight to the goal with a purpose in every step. I fight to win. I'm not just shadowboxing or playing around. Like an athlete I punish my body, treating it roughly, training it to do what it should, not what it wants to. Otherwise I fear that after enlisting others for the race, I myself might be declared unfit and ordered to stand aside.

1 CORINTHIANS 9:24-27, TLB

What we have covered in this book are lessons that focus on the beautiful and simple truth that God loves us and has provided a simple way to live an abundant and peaceful life. This is done by confessing our sins quickly and asking the Holy Spirit to control our lives. If you miss the simplicity of this truth, reading this book has been a waste of your time.

Seeing the lasting results in my own life and the lives of thousands of others over the last forty years has convinced me beyond any doubt that the Spirit-controlled Christian life is a miraculous experience. As long as I keep my sins confessed and ask the Holy Spirit to cleanse and fill me as often as necessary, the miracle continues.

Although I hesitate to use the word "magic" or miracle, the Holy Spirit does work miracles in our lives when we turn our lives over to God beyond anything we could do ourselves. Even now, after seeing so many lives changed over the years, the results of the Holy Spirit working in people's lives still constantly amaze me!

Over the years I have found several tools that have helped me find a biblical basis for my faith and the change in my life.

There was a lot of changing to do. Some changes were instantaneous and final; the urge to drink and swear just left and never returned. Other changes were more gradual and inconsistent; unselfishness, a servant attitude, compassion, experiencing the fruit of the Spirit. Consistency in Bible study and prayer also ranged from eagerness to nothing at all.

Bible memorization, Bible meditation, and the daily relationship with Christ have been the most helpful activities that have sustained me. Researching topics in the Bible has been a close second. A serious effort to understand the Bible was inspired by a fellow engineer who wanted to know how I changed my behavior at work. The challenge of giving him an answer got me started researching biblical topics. My pastor suggested that I get a "concordance."

I picked a few words to look up just for practice. Love was used in at least 1,000 verses. Peace was used in at least 700 verses. In the years to come, next to the Bible, a concordance proved to be the most helpful tool I ever used to discover what was in the Bible.

The first question on my mind: Why study the Bible? I opened the concordance to look up the word, Bible. What a surprise! The word Bible is not used in the Bible. I quickly learned there were other words: commandments, Word, Scripture, written Law, Word of God, teaching, precept.

I discovered there are hundreds of verses in the Bible that describe the Bible. I looked them all up; this took several months. I am not suggesting that there is a short-cut to knowing the God of the Bible. In the process I received the answer to my question about God. I discovered that the way to understand a topic is to find as many Bible verses as possible about the topic. The Bible is the best single commentary on itself.

What is your current method for studying the Bible? _____

_____

_____

Do you rely more on other books that speak about the Bible or on the Bible?

_____

Respond to this statement. It is easy to consume your time with books written explaining the Bible rather than reading the inspired Word of God! _____

_____

_____

_____

As a beginning Bible researcher, some ideas developed as I went along:

♦ Looking up verses helped me become familiar with the books of the Bible.

♦ Some verses leap out at you, some don't.

♦ Take your time. When a verse stands out, take a few minutes to think about it.

♦ If you have a day when the verses are "dead," quit for the day.

♦ Some days I had only fifteen minutes to work, other days several hours. There is no hurry.

♦ I developed my own personal concordance of verses that were especially meaningful to me.

The process of writing or typing out these verses helped fix them in my mind.

I have researched many, many topics. I will list some of them: God's resources, prayer, love, guidance or God's will, comfort and peace, power, sowing and reaping, sin, marriage, parenting, freedom, suffering.

You can add or subtract to such a list. As I attempted to learn more about the Bible, I worked on developing more than one topic at a time. I was catching on to the idea of meditating day and night.

I put topical headings on three-by-five cards and carried them around with me because I was learning that verses pertaining to my topics popped up in unexpected places. The most common place was the pastor's sermon. There were other places: at dinner, over the radio or TV, in a magazine article, in a book, or newspaper articles.

One topic that has been especially valuable to me is "God knows the heart." I will use that topic to illustrate how my procedure developed.

God Knows the Heart

2 Timothy 2:22	**Hosea 9:16**
1 Peter 3:4, 3:15	**1 Thessalonians 2:4**
Deuteronomy 4:28–31 6:5	**Isaiah 51:7**
Matthew 18:35	**Luke 8:15**
Psalm 95:10	**Psalm 38:8**

On a three-by-five card I wrote "God knows the heart." When I heard a verse used or read on this subject, I wrote down the reference.

After accumulating a group of references, I transferred them to a loose-leaf notebook and made a brief description like a concordance. It looked like this:

God Knows the Heart

- 2 Timothy 2:22—Call on God out of a pure heart.
- 1 Peter 3:4—Hidden man of heart to be meek and quiet.
- 1 Peter 3:15—Sanctify God in heart.
- Deuteronomy 4:28–31—Find God when search with whole heart.
- Deuteronomy 6:5—Keep word in heart.
- Matthew 18:35—Forgive from the heart.
- Psalm 95:10—Israelites erred in heart.
- 1 Thessalonians 2:4—God tries the heart.
- Isaiah 51:7—Law in heart removes fear.
- Luke 8:15—Nothing secret to God.
- Psalm 38:8—Roar because of a disquiet heart.

The list under this topic numbers over one hundred verses. Another step is to rearrange the references in the order they appear in the Bible.

There are books that have Bible verses already arranged for you. An example is the Thompson Chain Reference Bible It's a wonderful Bible to use and to study; the topics are well worth the time.

I recommend this method to the one who is unfamiliar with the Bible. Most importantly, I learned to use the Bible and to fix the verses in my mind. The process of writing out a Bible reference with a one-sentence description of the verse helped me to fix the content in my mind. Later on, I would scan those one-liners as I added to the list. A quick review occasionally has been like a drink of cold water to a thirsty pilgrim.

Long ago I learned that I didn't need to argue with anyone about God, His plan, His peace, or His joy that is available to all of us. I cannot make choices for anyone other than myself. If someone wants to be miserable, that is their choice. I am not going to try to talk them out of their misery.

At this time I know that I am approaching the finish line of my race. And today, if I had a choice, I would not choose to go back and start life over again. I eagerly look forward to meeting Jesus and many good friends in heaven.

If I go before you, I would like to be holding the tape when you finish the race God has given you to run.

Now I live each day so that I am ready to cross my own finish line.

Examine the Scriptures and/or your answers in today's lesson. Determine the most meaningful thought for you today. Write your thought for the day here:

_____

_____

_____

Applying what God is pointing out to you is essential. How will you apply this truth to your life today? _____

_____

_____

Write a short prayer to God that summarizes your thoughts._____

_____

_____

_____

Did God bring to mind someone who needs to hear this truth? Who?_____

_____

Thought for the Day:
Lasting change comes from a foundation built on Biblical faith.

◆

(Optional—But Recommended!)

Bring forward your thoughts from each day:

1. _____
2. _____
3. _____
4. _____
5. _____

Bring forward your application:

1. _____
2. _____
3. _____
4. _____
5. _____

Bring forward your prayers:

1. _____
2. _____
3. _____
4. _____
5. _____

Bring forward who you shared your thoughts with:

1. _____
2. _____
3. _____
4. _____
5. _____

Thought for the Week:

Everyone can finish the race of life a winner if they put the kingdom of God first.

◆

APPENDIX

Additional Verses
That Define Sin

If you show partiality, you commit sin, and are convicted by the law as transgressors. (JAMES 2:9) NKJV

To him who knows to do good and does not do it, to him it is sin. (JAMES 4:17) NKJV

He who despises his neighbor sins, but blessed is he who is kind to the needy. (PROVERBS 14:21) NIV

Rebellion is as the sin of witchcraft, and stubbornness is as iniquity and idolatry. (1 SAMUEL 15:23) NKJV

The wicked are like the tossing sea, which cannot rest, whose waves cast up mire and mud. "There is no peace," says my God, "for the wicked." (ISAIAH 57:20–21) NIV

There are six things the Lord hates, seven that are detestable to Him:

1. Haughty eyes
2. A lying tongue
3. Hands that shed innocent blood
4. A heart that devises wicked schemes
5. Feet that are quick to rush into evil
6. A false witness who pours out lies
7. A man who stirs up dissension among brothers. (See Prov. 16–19)

Whoever hates his brother is a murderer, and you know that no murderer has eternal life abiding in him.
(1 JOHN 3:15) NKJV

You have heard that it was said to those of old, You shall not commit adultery. But I say to you that whoever looks at a woman to lust for her has already committed adultery with her in his heart.
(MATTHEW 5:27–28)

We all, like sheep, have gone astray; each of us has turned to his own way; and the Lord has laid on him the iniquity of us all.
(ISAIAH 53:6) NIV

If you have bitter envy and self-seeking in your hearts, do not boast and lie against the truth. This wisdom does not descend from above, but is earthly, sensual, demonic. For where envy and self-seeking exist, confusion and every evil thing will be there.
(JAMES 3:14–16) NKJV

Your iniquities have separated between you and your God, and your sins have hid his face from you, that he will not hear.
(ISAIAH 59:1–2) KJV

She will bring forth a Son, and you shall call His name Jesus, for He will save His people from their sins.
(MATTHEW 1:21) NKJV

Blessed is he whose transgression is forgiven, whose sins are covered.
(PSALMS 32:1) KJV

ENDNOTES

Unit 2
1. *Fort Collins News,* Fort Collins, Colo. (Oct. 28, 1989), 1E.

Unit 3
1. *Time,* Beninga and Spradley, "The Burnout of Almost Everyone" (Sept. 21, 1981), 84.
2. S. I. McMillen, M.D., *None of These Diseases* (Waco, Tex: Word, n.d.), 64–65.

Unit 8
1. Billy Graham, *Till Armageddon* (Minneapolis, Minn.: Grason, 1981), 140.
2. Ibid., 9–10.
3. Ibid., 139.

Unit 9
1. Jay Carty, *Counter Attack* (Portland, Oreg.: Multnomah, 1988), 59–63.
2. Frederick Bueckner, *Wishful Thinking: A Theological ABC* (New York: Harper & Row, 1973), n.p.
3. P. T. Young, *Feelings and Emotions* (Englewood Cliffs, N.J.: Prentice-Hall, 1975), 138.
4. Marilyn Manning and P. A. Haddock, "Temper Those Tantrums," *Sky,* (July 1989), 100–105.

Unit 10

1. "The Ship," author unknown, *Poems That Live Forever*, Hazel Felleman, ed. (Doubleday, 1965).

Unit 11

1. William Shakespeare, *Hamlet*, act 3, scene 3, line 97–99.
2. *Chapel News*, a newspaper by Knute Larsen, The Chapel, 135 Fir Hill, Akron, OH 44304.
3. Ruth Paxton, *Wealth, Walk, Warfare of the Christian* (Old Tappan, N.J.: Fleming Revell, 1939), n.p.

Unit 12

1. *Time* (Sept. 19, 1990), 49–50.